STING
AND I

STING
AND I

The Totally Hilarious Story of Life as Sting's Best Mate

JAMES BERRYMAN

JOHN BLAKE

Published by John Blake Publishing Ltd,
3, Bramber Court, 2 Bramber Road,
London W14 9PB, England

www.blake.co.uk

First published in paperback in 2005

ISBN 1 84454 107 X

British Library Cataloguing-in-Publication Data:

A catalogue record for this book is available from the British Library.

Design by www.envydesign.co.uk

Printed in Great Britain by Bookmarque Ltd, Croydon, Surrey

1 3 5 7 9 10 8 6 4 2

Papers used by John Blake Publishing are natural, recyclable products
made from wood grown in sustainable forests. The manufacturing
processes conform to the environmental regulations of the country of
origin.

Plate section from the author's collection, except p5 and p6, top,
© Richard Young / Rex

Jim is creative and deserves to be doing something like this.
Crap book, mind – absolutely terrible!
STING

For Jennifer
Who wouldn't take 'no' for an answer

FOREWORD

J im Berryman once told me, after a particularly bad
day at the racetrack, that he felt so low he wanted to
hang himself and asked would I lend him the money so
he could buy himself the rope. As I had already funded
many of his previous failures, indeed positively heroic
failures as a bookie, I had no faith that he would pull
this one off either. I declined, told him to give up the
horses and do something creative, like needlepoint or
writing. 'Hell, you could always spin a good yarn when
you needed to borrow a few quid. Why don't you write
about yourself, or me, for that matter? None of the
clowns who've written biographies about me have ever
even met me. They get their "facts" from tabloids.
You've known me for 35 years; you couldn't do
any worse!'

Why didn't I keep my big mouth shut? I never thought he'd do it, but here it is on my desk, a big, fat manuscript from the fat ex-grammar schoolboy, ex-bookie, ex-bon-vivant and man-aboot-the-toon, who has lightened up my life with his humour and darkened my doorstep with his tales of woe for more years than any self-respecting pop star should sensibly admit to. So here's the book and, as to its veracity, I can only say that there's enough truth here for me to wish I'd lent him the money for the rope after all. Oh well...

Love and God bless all of you,

ACKNOWLEDGEMENTS

Huge gratitude to Peter, who never gave 'no' for an answer. Special thanks to the Hewsons and the Clerksons and also Ron White, Joyce White, Jim Veitch, Dave Bradshaw, Terry Wilkin and Anita Sumner. Finally, Jim and Irene, my mam and dad.

CONTENTS

INTRODUCTION

I gazed down into the blue-green waters of the outdoor swimming pool. It was approaching 2.00am, and some of the revellers at the lavish party at Sting's Country Seat, Lake House in Wiltshire, had dropped their inhibitions and were enjoying a dip. A suave American, who I had been introduced to earlier, joined me at the poolside.

'What do you think? Are you going in?' he asked.

'No, I don't think so. I haven't brought my cozzie, and I'm not going in naked. I couldn't stand the derision, and this dinner jacket is hired. I have no intention of ruining it,' I answered.

'Sting's a great guy, isn't he?' he remarked.

I wasn't going to argue, but couldn't resist trying to be funny. 'Yep, he sure is. Every November fifth, we stick him on the bonfire, but he always manages to wriggle out of it.'

'You do what?' he asked, totally oblivious to my jibe.

'Sorry, English joke. Not very funny.'

Before he could respond, another American joined us. 'You two look like you're ready to take the plunge,' he said, nodding towards the swimming pool.

It was the first Yank's turn for the wisecrack. 'We were,' he said to the second, smaller man, 'but I think he's already married.'

'I'm not, actually,' I told him. 'But it wouldn't work out. I have too many disgusting habits. Though I am very flattered, of course.'

'They all say that,' the first Yank said, moving off. 'See you later.'

They both departed, so I picked up another glass of Krug. I was more used to Newcastle Brown Ale. I lived in Newcastle, on a housing estate, and didn't have a brass farthing. The first American was Tom Hanks, the second, Dustin Hoffman. What the hell was I doing there with them? It's a long story…

1 – FIRST-DAY NERDS

'*Bad To Me*', Billy J Kramer and the Dakotas' latest hit, sang out from my bedside transistor radio. It was late August in 1963 and Billy J was making me think that I was sad and lonely. On this particular day, I also had good reason for thinking someone might be bad to me. I had been told there was trouble in store.

I called out, 'Mam?'

Silence.

'Mam!' Still no answer.

'What on earth do you want?' my mother finally replied, adding, 'And keep your noise down or you'll wake the baby.'

'I've got something to tell you, Mam. It's very important,' I announced sternly.

'I haven't got the time and neither have you,' she countered.

'I'm not going,' I whispered, but with as much purpose as I could muster.

'You're not going where?' she answered as she carefully took my new school uniform from the wardrobe. She laid it on my bed alongside the rest of my new clothes, all neatly set out for me. It was the first day of term at my new school – St Cuthbert's Grammar School, which was about six miles away from where we lived. The new school stood in the West End of Newcastle upon Tyne, whereas home was in a council housing estate, Longbenton, just north of the city. I had lived there almost all my life.

'I'm not going to school. I don't want to go to St Cuthbert's. Please don't make me, Mam,' I pleaded.

'Look, stop playing silly buggers. Don't be so daft. Put your new school uniform on this minute,' she insisted, then softened. 'You look really smart in it, you know. You'll feel a whole lot better when you're dressed. Come on, son, please.'

I was adamant. 'No, Mam, I'm not going and you can't make me.'

'*Oh, can't I*?' she spat back with equal conviction.

'No, you can't. I'm not going anywhere. You don't know what it's like at that place. Michael Walsh told me that the new boys have their heads flushed down the toilet. Some boys, the ones with ginger hair, get thrown over the rugby posts. Last year, they nailed a first year to the staff-room door by his ear! When the door opened, he swung inside, knocked over a tea urn and scalded the

Escapology teacher. When they took the kid down, his ear was over a foot long. They nicknamed him "Bunny". It's true, Mam.'

My mother looked at me impassively as I told the wild tale, my face funereal.

'I've never heard so much nonsense in my life. It must be a very funny school if they have an "Escapology" teacher. If it was Michael that told you all this, he's only pulling your leg. Come on, man. You can't be late on your first day.'

I sat down on my bed, folding my arms in defiance.

'Look, son, you have got to go to school. It's against the law if you don't. I'll have to go to prison if you refuse. Did you think of that?' she argued.

'Oh, you'll only get about six months at the most,' I sobbed back at her.

'*Put your bloody uniform on. Now!*' she screamed at me, miffed at the thought that I would rather she went to jail than I went to school.

All in all, she was putting up much stiffer opposition than I had anticipated. I half-heartedly started to dress, gently sighing. My mother left my room to attend to my baby sister Elaine, who had been woken by the furore.

There was someone at the door. Michael Walsh was a fourth-year student at St Cuthbert's and he was going to accompany me to school that first morning. It was he who'd filled my head with stories about 'Bunny' and the like, so when he told me, under further cross-examination, that they might not be true after all, I perked up a bit. He had volunteered to help me face the music for the first time.

So there I was in my claret blazer, complete with school badge, grey trousers, grey shirt and socks, with a badly knotted claret-and-blue tie around my scrawny neck. Over my shoulder hung a stiff new haversack. When Michael saw this item, he immediately burst out laughing.

Disconcertingly, he quickly pointed out my error of judgement; my bag looked ridiculous. For a start, it only had one strap, a long one that snaked over my shoulder, leaving the container nestling against my backside. On reflection, it resembled an old gas-mask holder, or the kind of rucksack that shipyard workers used for their flask and sandwiches.

'Get rid of that monstrosity, before we set off, Jim, or you won't survive the first morning,' Michael wisely informed me, before calling at his house to sort me out with one of his old bags. There was more to come.

'By the way, Jim, take that silly school cap off your head. Only kids on their first day or complete twozzers ever wear caps.' I did as I was told, then we were off to start, what was for me, a new life behind iron gates.

It was hard to say who shed more tears, my mother or I, as I waved her goodbye. For some weeks previously, I had felt that I wasn't going to like my new place of education. St Stephen's, my old primary school, was less than a quarter of a mile from home, a distance I could walk every day. Now I was being asked to travel several miles, by train and by bus, to St Cuthbert's. The thing was I hated new routines and long journeys – and, in my book, six miles was a very long way indeed.

As Michael and I neared the school, my 12-year-old frame filled with trepidation. Older boys looked me up and down, eyeing my new uniform with malice. I was fortunate on two counts, however. Firstly, I was with an older pupil and secondly – and much more importantly, as it turned out – I had not been so silly as to be caught wearing short trousers, like some other unsuspecting first-years. They paid for this almost certainly mother-inspired lunacy with whistles and catcalls as their lily-white knees came under the most rigorous inspection.

Once through the school gates for the first time, the sheer size of the place was daunting. To the right of the driveway lay a full-sized cricket pitch in immaculate condition. At the bottom of the drive stood 'The House', a nineteenth-century structure. The priests who taught at the school lived in this building, which also contained the Chapel and the Headmaster's Study. A little way from 'The House' stood the main school building. Erected in the 1920s, it consisted of about twenty classrooms on either side of a narrow corridor leading to an old-fashioned hall, which was in turn lined by classes on each side. It was the 1960s and education was expanding. At the rear of the main building was a recently erected modern wing, complete with large assembly hall and adjacent Chemistry and Physics labs.

A few steps from the main building was the

playground, crowned by metal five-a-side goalposts at each end. To my eyes, it didn't look big enough to accommodate 1,200 or so potential players of lunchtime kick-arounds, and so it proved. Beyond the schoolyard were the main playing fields.

On these fields stood five full-size football pitches in descending order of merit. The best, whose hallowed turf was hardly ever played on, was at the top, nearest the school. Lowest down the pecking order, the last pitch boasted an enormous oak tree, positioned just to the left of the penalty-spot. Apparently the tree had been the leading goal-scorer in Under-13 games for many years.

An ancient gymnasium was sited next to the playing fields, and for my first year at the school it also doubled as the dining room while a new one was being built. The situation wasn't ideal. I learned that it was particularly important to be vigilant in the first Games lesson after lunch, as a squashed pea on the gym floor could have devastating consequences. Whether gym or dining room, the building seemed disastrously ill-equipped for either function.

I had a few more surprises coming on my first day in this brave new world. Once inside the school building, Michael dropped me like a hot potato. I was on my own now. I found what I thought was the correct classroom and stood outside it. I could see that I was not the only newcomer who looked and felt like an outcast. Many young faces were tear-stained and afraid. I could only gaze with wide eyes at the older boys. I found it impossible to believe that some of them were of school age. Many of them looked like they needed a shave, I mused to myself.

I remarked to a fellow sufferer, 'Look at him. Just get those great big "sideboards".'

My young friend nervously looked around for the furniture, then even more nervously moved slowly away from me. 'Oh absolutely, old chap,' he muttered as he left, thinking that I was hallucinating.

'Sideboards' we called them in Longbenton. 'Mutton-chop side whiskers' might perhaps have made more sense to this lad; they were becoming fashionable at the time.

I strolled past the short-trousered brigade hoping to find anyone who looked like they might not faint at the mention of the word 'fart'.

'Christ, I hate this place already,' I heard a kindred spirit say, and I immediately stuck to the utterer of these words like fluff to a boiled sweet.

'Is this "Form 1"?' I asked my fellow inmate, knowing full well that it wasn't.

He answered slowly in a kind of Western drawl, '*Yup*.'

'No, it isn't,' I said.

'So, whit yu asking me fur, stranger?' he replied.

'Are you pretending to be a cowboy?' I asked innocently.

'*Yup*,' he laughed.

'I've been doing it since I got here, and you're the first to notice. Well done,' the lad said to me.

I was shitting myself, and here was someone who didn't give a toss. I was well impressed.

'I'm sorry. I knew this wasn't "Form 1", but I just wanted to talk to someone who didn't seem to be speaking with a mouthful of gobstoppers.'

He laughed again and I felt at ease for the first time that day.

The lad was tall for his 12 years and fair-haired. He had a serious face, with a steady gaze that seemed at odds with his obvious sense of fun. Although so young, he was already handsome in a rugged way and looked two years older than the rest of the first-years I had seen that morning. His hair was longer than anyone else's and ended in an exaggerated quiff that was the height of 1960s fashion. His uniform looked out of place on him, hanging like an onion sack, but he didn't care. You could just tell.

He reflected, 'Yeah, there are a canny few toffee-nosed buggers knocking around here.'

'Not me, though,' I very quickly confirmed. 'I'm from Longbenton.'

'Wallsend,' the lad replied. We had already hit common ground. Wallsend was as working-class as Longbenton.

'My name's Jim, Jim Berryman.' I introduced myself to Blondie, poking out a hand that he took and shook warmly.

Curiously he appeared both cocky and nervous at the same time; his tie was already undone and he was chewing bubble gum, which we were about to learn was

8

tantamount to stabbing a nun – a veritable crime against God. 'Pleased to met you, Jim,' said the lad. 'My name's Gordon Sumner.'

The formalities over, we went on to agree what an absolute dump we thought the place was.

'What class are you in?' I asked the new boy.

'1C,' he replied.

'I'm in Form 1,' I said, disappointed that I would not be joining my new pal in class. The streaming for that first term was simply done alphabetically. With me being a 'B' and he an 'S', we would not be joining up just yet.

The school bell rang out to signal the start of a less than inspiring academic career for both myself and, as it turned out, the tall, fair-haired Wallsend kid, *the boy who would be Sting*.

'See you around, bonny lad,' said Sting going off to 1C. Little did I realise that we would be seeing each other around for the next forty-odd years – some of them very odd years.

2 – THE NAME GAME

By the end of that first day, my worst suspicions were confirmed: I did not like the school. And, judging by the age of some of the masters, there was no early retirement plan for the staff. Several looked absolutely ancient, well past pensionable age. Our Latin teacher, Mr Mulcahy, for instance, looked only a few days short of his telegram from the Queen. He was a pretty fair tutor despite his longevity. This presumably had something to do with the fact that the Romans were still on these shores when he was a lad. He needed to use a magnifying glass to mark our homework. I presumed that no one had told him that spectacles had been invented and I always pictured him marking our papers wearing a deerstalker hat.

However, it was not the antique Mr Mulcahy who had the dubious privilege of overseeing my first lesson at the school. That honour fell upon the broad shoulders of one

Mr Spoor, a Geography teacher. The first thing he wanted to do, not surprisingly, was to draw up a plan of the class and put everyone's name down on it. Head down, he started to ask each boy, in turn, his name. 'Back row first,' he commanded. 'No Christian names.' I looked forward to the usual array of ridiculous surnames that crop up when forty or so people are gathered together. Apart from 'Fishwick', which seemed to amuse some of the class, there were no silly names on the agenda. I had hoped someone might have been called 'Arsebone' or the like.

The taking down of names did not pass without incident, however. When I had first walked into class that morning, I had noticed a boy standing next to himself. On closer inspection the boy was, in fact, two boys – twin boys. Twin Scottish boys. Identical twin Scottish boys. I later discovered that they were called Gavin and Callum Barr. Like all good twins they were inseparable, so naturally they sat next to each other. Spoor went on his merry way.

'Bradshaw.'

'Right, next.'

The next boy replied, 'Bulman, sir.'

'OK. Bulman, is that with one "L", son?'

'Yes, one "L", sir,' said Joe Bulman, someone I still call my friend to this day.

'Next,' Spoor ploughed on.

'Barr,' said the first of the twins.

'Did I hear a sheep just then?' said the jovial master in a feeble attempt to be humorous. To be fair, it was one

12

of the better efforts that I was to hear over the years –
from the staff, anyway. The St Cuthbert's teachers were
never in much danger of causing their pupils injury
through excessive laughter. This time the class reacted
favourably with guffaws that could be heard a couple of
streets away.

'What did you say your name is, son?' Mr Spoor
kindly enquired.

'Barr,' answered the faintly bored new pupil.

'How do you spell that?' asked Spoor.

'T-H-A-T' came the riposte of the first Barr.

Spoor's jaw dropped as a ripple of chuckles ran
through the room. 'Listen, mister, if I want a comedian,
I'll go seek Arthur Askey,' snapped back the miffed
master, issuing a terrible threat to fetch the aged comic
to class.

'B-A-double R,' the young Scot resumed, deadpan.

The face-off apparently over, the master continued his
task. 'Next.'

Now for some fun, we all thought. Mr Spoor had
hardly looked up from his desk, and would not have
noticed that he was in for more of the same. Barr
Mk II took centre-stage. The second Barr, hoping to
differentiate himself from his brother, decided to break
one of the most important school rules, and unwisely
gave his Christian name as well as his surname. What the
lad did not appreciate was the fact that masters at the
school did not react to first names.

'Callum Barr,' answered the cool Caledonian.

'What?' asked 'Spooky', as we learned he was nicknamed.

'Callum Barr,' repeated the second of the twins.

'I know they call *him* "Barr", I want to know *your* name, if it isn't too much trouble,' the teacher thundered, waving vaguely in the twin's direction, though still not looking up.

Undeterred, the young Jock repeated his assertion. 'Callum Barr.'

Spoor glanced in his direction but still could not see what the rest of the room had already discerned. 'Callumbah! Are you by any chance African?' Spoor asked him. I presumed he was being serious.

'No, sir, I am not African, I am Scottish,' replied the pissed-off youth.

'Your name doesn't sound very Scottish to me,' Spooky insisted.

Barr II was not in the least bit perturbed. He calmly advised the befuddled man, 'On the contrary, sir, "Callum" is a very old traditional Scottish name.'

'Ah, so your name is "Callum". Why on earth didn't you say so before?' said the man, now happy with his handling of the idiotic Scots git.

What really astounded me over the next term was that Spoor never seemed to realise he had twins in his class or even that the Barrs were related for that matter. He always called the first one 'Barr' and the other one 'Callum', despite the fact few people could tell them apart. He was, I decided, either completely barmy or an absolute genius.

Mr Spoor, then, was in his mid-50s, stockily built, about five feet nine in height, with a decent head of hair, brown and wavy with just a tad of brilliantine, I guessed. With his care-worn face, he had, I thought, the typical look of a St Cuthbert's master. Institutionalised by years of devotion to hundreds of pupils, very few of whom ever gave a toss about glacial erosion or anything else to do with Geography. Indeed, he was rumoured to have worn the same check jacket every day for thirty years – even the leather patches on the elbows had leather patches. On top of this, he actually lived in a house that backed on to the school playing fields. Vindictive members of 3D would sneak into his garden and piss on his leeks.

On that first morn of the first day, Spoor must have already been reflecting on his bad luck: he was only a few minutes into the new term and he had already encountered the class sociopath. If he thought that this would be the end of the name trouble, he was sadly mistaken.

After a couple of bland names like 'Doona' and 'Elliot', more confusion reigned. 'Next,' he resumed.

'Yoyth,' the lad seemed to say.

'Right, next... What? Yoyth? Does that begin with a "Y", because if it does, you're in the wrong class, son,' Spoor advised, not seeming to notice that there was no such name in the whole world as 'Yoyth'.

The boy in the adjacent desk quickly piped up. 'His name is "Joyce", sir!'

But Spoor was having none of this. 'No first names! Wait a minute. "Joyce" is a girl's name! Are you trying to tell me that this person's name is "Joyce Yoyth"? Is that right?' Obviously the thought of having a transsexual on the school premises repulsed the staid master. He launched himself out of his seat to boldly confront the pervert, Joyce Yoyth.

Yoyth, however, was no juvenile transvestite, nor was he a girl. He was just a frightened little lad with a bad lisp. 'Yoyth, thur, YAY-OH-Y-THEE-EE,' the terrified kid spelled out as Spoor arrived within inches of his shaking body. 'Yoyth ith my thecond name,' Joyce asserted as the master drew back, his darkest fears dispelled.

'Oh, Joyce. I see now. Oh, God, what's the time? Is it four o'clock yet?'

It was twenty past nine.

Uncannily, sitting at the very next desk was a boy with another debilitating speech impediment. If Spoor was worried, thinking he would have to translate into English every word that Joyce said to him in the coming term, worse was to follow. 'Next.'

'Er, er, ehr, her, her, Heth, Hether, Hetherin, Hetherin, Hether, Heth, Hetherington, Ssssir,' the poor lad finally spluttered.

'No need to be nervous, son,' suggested Spoor, hoping against hope that nerves were the reason for this incredible bout of stammering.

'I'm n, n, n, not ner, ner, nervous,' stuttered the redoubtable Hetherington, a big red-faced boy, who I later found to be a smashing lad, as good as gold.

'I see,' said the resigned master, slowly losing the will to live.

The class naturally took great delight in the performance of the two unfortunate lads within their ranks. The presence of Joyce and Hetherington would greatly distract from our own shortcomings, not to mention wasting at least ten minutes of every lesson while translations took their toll.

More names were taken, then it was my turn. 'Berryman,' I called out, without, I thought, a trace of a lisp or stammer.

'Is that spelled with a "Y" or an "I"?' asked Spoor.

I thought that, after Joyce and Hetherington, he had taken leave of his senses. 'Er, neither, sir. It's spelled with a "B", sir.'

The class, who had listened to Joyce and Hetherington in virtual silence, now decided that this was the funniest thing they had ever heard. Howls of laughter were raised to the roof.

'Another comedian,' Spoor sighed.

I quickly understood what he had meant, and answered, 'With a "Y", sir,' too late to pacify the mob.

Spoor, now placated, must have had quite enough of his new pupils, who appeared to consist entirely of social misfits or wise guys. Each one of them was well prepared to make his life a misery, and he must have reflected that he had the homicidal 5D next lesson, who last term, when they were merely 4D, had tried to murder him with a cunning stunt involving a bucket of water and an electrified blackboard.

Although I was happy to blame the master for my faux pas, I was decidedly irked at break-time, when I discovered that the chat among the kids in 'Form 1' was not about the surly responses of the Barr twins, Joyce Yoyth or the world-class stammering of 'Hairy' Hetherington, but about that clot 'Berryman', with his 'spell it with a B' bit. I had started my days at St Cuthbert's the way I intended to continue – as a complete prat. At break-time I moved away from members of my own form, who were busy taking the piss out of me. The reason was that I had spotted my friend, Michael Walsh, who only a couple of hours earlier had chatted happily with me on our way to school.

'Hello, Mickey, all right?' I asked innocently.

Michael looked at me as if I was a turd. I was persona non grata. Having first-years calling you by your first name when you were a fifth-year was unheard of. Not that I knew. Michael didn't answer me, pretending I was referring to someone else.

He told me later that you could not have a friend outside your own year-group. I told him he should grow up, along with everyone else in the school. Strangely enough, he agreed with me. I told him that, in future, I would only speak to him in school if his arse were on fire. Another custom I found alien to me was that most of the pupils referred to each other by their surnames, just as the teachers did. I couldn't understand it. It was not as if we were at Eton College, for Christ's sake! I slunk away from

Michael, shocked by his snub, only to walk slap bang into the young lad I had met before classes.

'Hello, Sumner,' I greeted him, remembering his name and using the formality that seemed to be the norm.

Sumner apparently didn't think too much of my greeting, as he answered with a biting, 'What's with the "Sumner" business? I wasn't aware I was your friggin' butler.'

I was surprised, but pleased he didn't want us to refer to each other as 'Sumner' and 'Berryman', a practice as alien to me as grape-treading.

'Have you got any servants in Longbenton?' asked Sting.

'No, of course we haven't,' I told him.

'Well, you can call me Gordon, and I'll call you Berryman.' Then he gave that mischievous laugh of his that he still has to this day, though some might doubt it.

'Righto, Gordon,' I replied.

'Spiffing, Berryman. Go feed the hounds,' he said, making me laugh. Something that, only minutes earlier, I had thought I might never do again.

We continued our male bonding with a discussion of the daft names in our classes. He thought someone in his class was called 'Shitstick', whereas I told him of Joyce, 'Hairy' Hetherington and me. Because he was laughing with me and not at me, I felt a whole lot better. I was going to like this kid. The school bell sounded to signal the return to the fray. We promised to meet up again at lunchtime, though we could not dine together as we were kept with our own forms. After school, we met up outside and travelled together on the bus, chuntering on like we had known each other for years. At the railway station we parted company as we took different trains home.

'See you tomorrow, bonny lad,' I shouted after him.

'Cheerio, Berryman. Damn fine chap,' he hollered back.

I had made a new friend, but I still wasn't too keen on the school. When I arrived home, I could see that my mam had been crying. 'What's the matter, Mam?' I asked rather needlessly.

'I've been worried about you, haven't I? You didn't want to go, remember?' 'I'm sorry I upset you, Mam, but I think I was right. It's not a very nice school. A lot of the kids are right snobs.'

'How you can hate the place after just one day is beyond me,' she chided.

'Anyway, Mam, I've made a new friend. He's called Gordon Sumner, and he's a good laugh. He's from Wallsend, but we're not in the same form. Pity, but we get the same bus into town. He hasn't got a haversack like nearly all the other kids. He's got a black leather briefcase that he holds under his arm. Dead posh.'

'He's dead posh, and he comes from Wallsend?' she mocked.

'Nah, *he's* not posh, man. Just his briefcase,' I replied.

'So you will be going back tomorrow, will you?'

'I suppose so. Don't worry about prison,' I comforted her.

'All right, I won't, but you know you will have to stay at that school until you are at least 16, don't you?'

'Will you come and get me when I'm 16 then, Mam?'

'Oh, get away, you daft sod,' she countered.

I ate my tea, then changed into jeans and a T-shirt to join some ruffian pals on the back field for a game of football. They quizzed me on my first day at the grammar school, but I didn't say much, other than talk about my new mate.

On my second day at school, I went along with a heavy heart. It had seemed OK back home after the first day, but, when I realised that I would have to repeat the routine every day, I became even more depressed. In the ensuing weeks, I found out that St Cuthbert's was a highly complex seat of learning.

Young Sumner had made an impression on me in such a short time, if I had only known what was to become of him in later years I would have signed him up in a flash, although I think Sting's lawyers might have had something to say about the terms and conditions of the contract – albeit even if I did allow Sting five per cent, generous as I am.

I had accepted the fate that lay ahead at St Cuthbert's and, with my newfound friend, I felt a little easier about being able to handle such an arduous servitude – though, as it happens, it was the masters at St Cuthbert's that deserved medals the size of bin lids for tolerating our presence over the years to come. It was a large step for mankind – or so I thought – and like a lamb to the slaughter I accepted what all kids went through. Although I had the feeling I was special and it was only I who could be made to suffer in such a special way – others couldn't hold a candle to my pain – of course I was wrong.

Something important lay ahead of us. That first week we were introduced to the teachers who were to lead us into the first set of examinations at the end of that term, just before Christmas. These exams were important as they determined the stream in which you would spend the rest of your school life. The most able students in Form 1, the least accomplished in Form 1D. The majority in 1A, 1B and 1C.

3 – OLD MASTERS

After the bemused Mr Spoor and the antediluvian Mr Mulcahy, we met our new French master, Mr Kelly. A dapper little bloke in his 50s, rotund, with thinning Brylcreemed hair and horn-rimmed specs, he smiled a lot – not a trait recognisable among many St Cuthbert's staff. 'Ned Kelly', as he was inevitably nicknamed, always wore a smart blue suit and had a Gallic swagger about him that we all admired. He also called the boys 'Mister', which made us feel more like grown-ups. He used to tell us that he wanted everything to be 'in apple-pie order', and I don't think many of us let him down. We picked up the language pretty quickly considering that most of us had never been taught a foreign language before.

Our English teacher was Brian Noon, or 'Twelve o'clock' as we rather predictably monikered him. A slightly built guy, only in his early-30s at the time, he was positively a child in the St Cuthbert's hierarchy. Like a lot of English teachers, he often appeared aloof and gave the impression that he fancied he was rather above teaching us snotty-nosed sods the deft nuances of the English language. I didn't take to him at all at first, but, when I found out that he was a keen Newcastle United supporter like myself, I suddenly viewed him in a new light. When my mate Joe Bulman later told me that he had spotted 'Noony' at Newcastle Central Station, hurling abuse at the fleeing Sunderland fans after a local derby match, he almost became deified. Despite this, I did particularly badly in English that term. It was obviously his fault, I argued to myself.

Mr Savage, the History teacher, was a man of about 50, who knew his stuff and was quite well liked, though he was not hard enough on the class, who would often take the mickey if given the chance. I never once heard him raise his voice. Mr Porter, our Physics master, had the useful knack of making what I considered to be a mind-numbing subject even more boring.

Mr Cutter, the Maths master, was a different kettle of fish. A fat little bloke with bulging, staring eyes, he was much more interesting. Balding with a sallow complexion, which turned purple when he was riled, he was the most able of men. Passionate about his subject and patient to a fault, he was a great communicator. He could often be genuinely humorous, but he also had a side to him that would unfailingly shut up the rowdiest of classes: a furious temper. His face would contort with fury as he howled his displeasure an inch from the terrified offender. For all that, he was well liked but no one ever deliberately tried to give him the opportunity to show off the 'Mr Hyde' side of his normal good nature.

The Chemistry teacher, 'Spike' Hughes, was a genuine eccentric. He was like a tall version of 'Harpo Marx'. He had a skinny frame and a somewhat pockmarked face. Unfortunately, for his pupils, Spike also had a party piece. He sought to demonstrate his mood swings by smiling, then passing the palm of his hand down his face to reveal a serious visage. He did it the other way round too, six or seven times a lesson. It was amusing once, but only once. By the end of that term, I could willingly have throttled the bastard. Being required to laugh every time he produced this masterpiece of comedy was making me nauseous.

Mr Hughes had a saying, which he repeated almost as often as his 'hilarious' face routine. He would pick up an implement, used for holding test tubes and chant, 'Do you know what we call these things? "Neepaz"? "Tweezaz"? "Peenchaz"? *No*! They are *tongs*! What are they?' The class would then have to repeat his maxim in unison – again, relatively amusing when heard by 12-year-olds for the first time. After 600 repeats, I think we were quite entitled to tell old Spike that, if he ever said that to us again, we would be obliged to put his knackers in a clamp, gradually increasing the pressure until he gave his solemn oath that he would never again subject his class to his warped, repetitive attempts to amuse. He was a very daft old chemist and I actually can't remember a sodding thing about Chemistry, except that those things you pick test tubes up with are called, I think, 'peenchaz' or possibly 'tweezaz'.

Our Religious Education teacher was Fr Duffy. RE was not just another subject at St Cuthbert's; it was a way of life. It was expected, for instance, that a proportion of the pupils would become priests in the normal course of events. Oddly enough, lessons in Religious Education were almost incidental to the Catholic regime that operated throughout the school with the paradoxical result that no one took them seriously.

Fr Duffy was a young priest, who was even more nervous than his pupils. We instinctively sensed that he was a newcomer to the teaching game, so he gained all the respect his position called for... precisely none! We used to lead him a merry dance, asking him questions about sex and these were as alien to him as they were to us. He used to blush as red as a postman's van. He took it in good spirit though, and we admired him all the more for it. When someone asked him, 'Father, what's an erection?' he merely replied, 'Well, the Eiffel Tower is a very large one.'

Last but not least, there was our Games teacher, Stan Eardley. Known simply as 'Stan' by kids and teachers alike, he did not seem to age by a single day during my seven years at the school, or for that matter ever change his clothes. He wore his uniform of cream shirt under a white cricket jumper, with orange tracksuit bottoms and old-fashioned baseball boots, for every lesson.

When young, we used to play football on the ridiculous

pitch with the gigantic oak tree. The ball often smacked into it, not to mention the odd body doing likewise. The trials for the first-year football team held in this most bizarre of settings were little more than farcical. I was amazed to be picked for the side, as I had stood behind said tree, reading a copy of *The Eagle* comic, for almost the whole game. Stan was a good judge though, and I was never dropped from the school side until, with the ravages of alcohol, I lost my place in the First XI.

When I met young Sting again, we compared notes on our teachers and concluded that not many of them were able to command our undivided attention. As we became friendlier, we started to discuss just about every subject under the sun. What puzzled me a bit was the fact that he always carried with him an enormous tome written by philosophers, the names of whom meant nothing to me – 'Kierkegaard' read one, and another 'Emanuel Kant'. Sting never spoke of philosophy, so I remained philosophical about his reasons for towing the books about with him. In later years, I asked him what this had all been about. 'I can't remember. I suppose I was just a poser' was all I could glean from him.

If he wasn't lumping heavy books about, he would have a long-playing record stuffed under his arm. 'The Rolling Stones', one read. *Never heard of them*, I mused. As we were not allowed to play records at school, I never did figure out why he always had one with him. Posing again, perhaps? He appeared to be a bit of a loner and, the more I got to know him, the more I realised that, although we were good pals, there was another side to him that was difficult to work out. He was not just like the rest of us. Sometimes argumentative and morose but mostly good-natured and lively, 'moody' was as good a description for him as any.

We sat our exams in December, and our similarly average marks put us in the same form, 1A, the second-top stream. Not too bad a performance, we agreed. Although I had made some good pals in Form 1, notably Paul Doona and Joe Bulman, I was quite happy to be in the same form as the young Sting. We soon arranged to sit next to each other in class.

4 – JAMES EDWARD, THE CONFESSOR

Neither Sting nor I were very religious, although I had been an altar boy at my local church of Sts Peter and Paul in Longbenton. What I absolutely abhorred was the Catholic practice of confession. I told Sting how much I hated telling someone about all the mischief I had been up to. As it was always the same priest who heard my confession, he always knew that it was my confession he was listening to, which was why he would often glare at me afterwards, or so I thought. 'Where's the anonymity?' I argued to Sting, not that it mattered much really.

In any case, I was not exactly a sinner on any great scale, my worst transgression being the neglect of my pet hamster – not exactly a garrotting offence. Although I only ever ran off a string of routine misdemeanours, I was so concerned that the parish priest knew who I was that I would go to extraordinary lengths to disguise my true identity. For instance, I would put on different accents in order to throw the priest off the track. Unfortunately, they never seemed to work. After one confession, which I had rasped out in a thick cockney accent – I was quite expert at putting this on due to the fact that my dad was born within the sound of Bow Bells – the priest concluded, 'Thank God for a good confession and for your penance say three "Our Fathers" and three "Hail Marys" please, Jim!'

Despite my attempts at deception, he could pick me out as the sinner first time. This could only be because, no matter how hard I tried to disguise my voice, I always had the same catalogue of minor sins to reel off. He knew it was me by the constant repetition. I quickly developed a plan: I must not repeat myself; I must not repeat myself. I told Sting of my problem and his answer was straight and to the point: 'Think of some different sins to confess, you divvy.'

Easier said than done. I was only 12. And apart from missing the odd morning prayer, I didn't get the opportunity to sin that much which made it all the more ridiculous that I should want to hide my identity in the first place. Adolescents are rarely logical, however, so Sting tried to help.

'Don't you hang around with a bunch of hooligans at home?' he asked.

'Yes' I replied. 'What the bloody hell has that got to do with it?'

'This foolish act is, in fact, a sin,' he announced with all the authority of the Pope.

'I only have the odd game of football with the lads. That can't be a sin surely? We don't go round coshing old grannies, or pinching their raspberry ruffles!'

'My parish priest told me that, if you had so-called pals who were non-Catholics and they led you astray, this was the sin of "Keeping bad company". You have, I reckon, committed this heinous sin on dozens of occasions, have you not?' Sting informed me.

I agreed with this nonsense and decided to admit to involvement in the gross act of 'Keeping bad company' at my next confession.

'Bless me, Farther, for oi haf sint; it is tree wakes sins moy last carnfeshun,' I opened in my best Irish brogue. I rolled out some of the usual stuff, then threw in the 'bad company' bit.

'Ah, you have kept bad company, excellent,' the priest purred. 'Non-Catholics, of course, trying to make you miss mass and swear, no doubt,' he continued.

He must know these lads personally, I thought to myself.

'That's right, Father, demons they are,' I went on, slightly overdoing it and forgetting the accent.

'Thank God for a good confession, and will you take a decade of the rosary as penance. Get me a "Football Pink", will you, please, Jim?' The old sod still knew it was me and not only that: he now knew I kept 'bad company'.

This was a disaster. That bloody idiot Sumner. I'll get him for this! I thought. By the time I got back to school, I had mellowed. I only wrote 'FUCK OFF' on the back of Sting's

31

English notebook, which he expertly changed to the more mundane, if even more puzzling, 'BOOKING OFFICE'. I shall have to remember that one, I thought.

'It was no use, I take it?' Sting needlessly asked me, waving his notebook in my face. 'Look, just change your priest. Go to confession here at school if you're so bothered,' he advised.

This was either a brain wave, or a brainstorm. Confessions were held in the school chapel every lunchtime, with some 1,200 boys, potential penitents, all reeling off the same sins. Anonymity preserved, perfect! Sting was a genius. School confession it was then. I asked Sting to come with me for moral support. After I'd given him an 'Indian burn', he willingly agreed.

On 11 October 1964, Sting and I trooped to school confession. To this day, I do not know which one of the priests it was who listened to the baring of my soul. Going by the voice, I have my suspicions but I'll leave it at that. Sting went in first and was out again within a matter of minutes. He didn't sin much, he told me. He may have made up for it since then, however. It was now my turn.

'Bless me, Father, for I have sinned. It is two weeks since my last confession.' I dropped the Indian accent I was intending to use as Sting had pointed out there weren't any Indian boys at the school. I might have stood out too much or, worse, the priest might have thought I was taking the piss.

I was happy to note that, covering the confession-box grille into which you spoke, there was a thick purple cloth between saint and sinner. This made it impossible for the priest to recognise me. I had a streaming cold that day and I had a deep voice for a 12-year-old, so I would have sounded a lot older than I actually was. This was to prove crucial in the unfolding drama. After all, it wasn't only pupils who went to these confessions but masters as well. Indeed some were sitting in the chapel waiting their turn, while I knelt before the priest. Confusion was about to reign yet again.

To my consternation, the priest was talking far too loudly. I had heard almost every word the priest had hollered at Sting and so could everyone else in the pews. Although I was whispering my sins, he boomed out his replies for all to hear. 'You have kept bad company,' he bellowed so loudly that people must have heard his words down on the schoolyard.

'Does this mean that you have broken the Seventh Commandment?' he shouted. He had me stumped there. I would not have chosen the Ten Commandments as my specialist subject, if ever asked to compete on *Mastermind*. I thought about poking my head out of the confessional and asking the congregation if anyone knew what the Seventh Commandment might entail. That seemed a trifle extreme. I fancied that it might be the one about coveting your neighbour's ox. But, as far as I knew, no one in Longbenton owned an ox. The people two doors away from us kept a pig in a tea chest by the fire but I wasn't sure if that counted. Anyway, what did 'covet' mean? If it meant 'ride' as I thought it might, I was on safe ground. I had never ridden an ox or a pig in my life. My next thought was simply to leave: to get up and walk out. I quickly rejected this notion. Not only could Sting put the finger on me, but so could several members of staff. I took the nutter's way out.

'Yes, Father,' I said in a low deep voice. 'I have broken the Seventh Commandment,' despite not knowing what on earth it was. The Seventh Commandment, I now know, is 'Thou Shalt Not Commit Adultery'. But not many 12-year-olds have had the honour of committing this act and I was no exception. After a theatrically audible cough, the priest pressed on with relish.

'How many times have you committed this sin, my son?' he continued. He was still shouting.

Only thinking that I had been involved with a few Protestant ruffians, I replied, 'Nearly every night after school and just about all day Saturdays and Sundays.'

He gave out a gasp that could have been detected out on the playing fields. 'Jesus, Mary and Joseph, you should be ashamed,' he screamed. 'Is this a married person you are involved with?' He continued to shout, making sure, I suppose, it was genuine adultery I was into, not mere fornication.

'No, none of them are married,' I answered completely truthfully.

'None of them!' he bawled, recoiling in horror at what he had discovered.

'*Just how many people are you involved with*?' he demanded.

As I had several mates who were my so-called 'bad company', I answered with veracity, 'About ten altogether, Father.'

'Ten! You are seeing ten different women all at the same time?'

I was unable to take all this in. I could hear laughter coming from outside as everyone could hear the distraught priest ranting on about ten women of easy virtue who were pandering to every whim of the pre-teenage stud. I decided to put him right once and for all.

'Yes, about ten altogether but different ones on different nights. But only all ten together, perhaps, at the weekend when I have more time.' My parish priest had never made all this fuss. Then it dawned on me that the priest had mentioned women. I presumed he meant girls so I tried putting him at his ease. 'By the way, Father, there are no females involved; they are all just young lads from the housing estate.' Judging by the awful noise he made, I thought he was going to peg out on the spot.

'Arggghhh… young boys from a housing estate. Are you telling me you are having sex with young boys, every night of the week and all day at weekends? How can I give you Absolution? I should have you removed from the school immediately and you should be punished for those gross sins by a long period of imprisonment. May you roast in the fiery flames of Hell. Now get out!'

Mention of the word 'sex' early on in his diatribe had put me on my guard. Whatever it was we got up to after school, sex was definitely not part of it. Surely having some unsavoury pals did not deserve all this mayhem. I started to whimper, 'Please, Father, I don't like girls. I don't know very much about sex. Perhaps I have not broken the Seventh Commandment...'

'Do you know what the Seventh Commandment is?' he enquired.

'N-no, Father, it's not about oxen or pigs, is it?'

He gave out an almighty groan and again I could hear raucous laughter from outside the confessional.

'All right, don't cry,' he said, softening. 'Thank God for a... er, good confession. Say three decades of the rosary for your penance and please don't come to me again. I have a bad heart.'

When I finally rose from my knees and hurried from his torture box, I was met with a round of applause from the waiting kids and teachers alike. Some of them, Sting in particular, were crying with laughter. I knelt down to say my hefty penance, vowing to myself to plot awful revenge on the boy Sting whose fucking stupid idea it had been in the first place. He further annoyed me by telling all and sundry about this episode of high farce. He has also called on me to repeat the tale to dozens of strangers over three decades. I am still awaiting my revenge. Be warned, Sting!

5 – ROD STEWARD

Fr Walsh was a stern-looking sod. Before I had attended St Cuthbert's, priests had always appeared to me as jovial, avuncular people – old duffers who did not have an unkind word to say about anyone. Fr Walsh was not like that. Balding and granite-faced, he never smiled and curiously only seemed to have two duties to perform: to ring the school bell as and when required and to beat the living shit out of anyone unlucky enough to have been sent to him for punishment.

Every pupil at the school – even my older friend Michael Walsh, his namesake, who as far as I knew had an exemplary record – had at one time had the privilege of being sent to the punishment master. There always seemed to be a reason, no matter how trivial, for a trip to his office. The pupil was then treated to three, four, five or, in extreme cases, say for spitting at the caretaker, six of the best. These were heavy strokes of the cane across the backside, but not the bare backside as has been reported in some previous accounts. This was a school, not a Japanese work camp. At the time, I was in the habit of confusing the term 'capital punishment' with 'corporal punishment'. It's just as well Fr Walsh was not under the same misapprehension, or there would have been no pupils left at the school come the fifth-year! Caning was a way of life at the school, and the boy Sting and I, even at such an early age, had our fair share of thrashings.

My first encounter with the four-foot rod was in our first year. What had I done to deserve this belting, poisoned the Head Boy's pet iguana or something equally heinous? No, I had committed a far more serious offence. I had torn a page from my English notebook. Send for the firing squad! While doing my homework, I had an accident, spilling ink on to the pristine page of the notebook. Then I removed the spoiled page and threw it away.

This villainous act came to light when Mr Noon, our English teacher, was returning our exercise books after marking our homework. As he was about to toss my book back to me, he suddenly froze in mid-throw. He placed the book on the palm of his hand, expertly weighing it. It was a quarter of an ounce light. He could tell. Then he put it next to his ear and flicked the pages. In an instant, his ears had confirmed his first suspicions. Fifty-one pages were present; one was missing. He looked at me with malice, sternly announcing, 'You have stolen a page from this school book. Go to Fr Walsh immediately.' I just sat there smiling. He was some joker, this bloke. I sat stock-still. 'Go, now!' he commanded. I still never moved, although the joke was starting to wear a bit thin. 'Do I have to drag you there myself, you stupid child?' he snapped, his face too serious for this to be an elaborate hoax.

I trudged off for my punishment. Full of trepidation, I knocked on Fr Walsh's study door, then entered. Surely when I told him why I was there, he would simply pat me on the head and send me back to class. Surely no action was needed over this small misunderstanding. In actuality, he caned me on the arse and sent me back to class. Moving gingerly away from his study with my bum stinging to three of the best, I wondered what would have happened if I had lost an entire notebook; I reckoned I might have been guillotined on the spot. Tearing a page from your notebook was obviously on a par with ripping the cassock from the back of a cardinal. When I told Sting about my thrashing, he laughed until he cried. A couple of days later, however, he got his comeuppance when we were involved in an offence that led us both to Fr Walsh.

Our joint transgression, this time, was that, without regard for the health or safety of others, with wanton abandon, we did climb aboard a train, on to a carriage forbidden to the blood-crazed savages of St Cuthbert's. It was a school rule that only the first two carriages on the train were to be used by St Cuthbert's pupils. Sting and I now travelled on the same train home as he had recently moved with his family to Tynemouth. On the day in question, we were late going home and had to run for the train. We only just made it, leaping into the last carriage. When this happened you were supposed to move to the designated front carriages at the next station stop, but we couldn't be arsed. Instead, we were sitting quietly on the coast train, probably discussing the merits of the Latin writer Pliny, when a prefect spotted us, took our names and told us to report to Fr Walsh first thing next morning. What a twat! Sting swore revenge on the prefect. A week later, the lad's briefcase was mysteriously filled with custard. Draw your own conclusions.

I could never understand why we were required to use the front two compartments on that train. There were never more than a half-a-dozen St Cuthbert's kids on the train. The head must have imagined three or four hundred ranting and raving lads swarming all over the train like it was the 'Benghazi Express'. He must have envisaged a scene from one of those daft St Trinians films, with kids hanging out of the windows, waving hockey sticks, cricket bats and chain-saws. Nothing could have been further from the truth. We were models of decorum.

As we walked to Fr Walsh's office, Sting asked me what I thought our punishment might be. I had just been beaten for the missing-page fiasco and he told me, straight-faced, that his last thrashing was because his dad was a milkman. It was obvious we would be saying hello to Mr Stick again. For our reckless and indeed dangerous act, we received four strokes of the lash. When Fr Walsh told us, 'Someone could have been killed on that train,' we thought the prefect must have reported us for carrying guns at the very least, as opposed to the truth.

I had now been unjustly beaten twice and Sting got into even more hot water. We were starting to become paranoid about it. Why would we next be caned? Would a prefect see us walking on a crack in the pavement? Would a master overhear one of us saying the word 'constipation' on a Holy day of obligation? It was anyone's guess. The list of things you could be whacked for was endless, though we did not repeat the mistake of 'dangerous train travel' as our last sin had been described.

It could be that the beating we endured together cemented our lasting friendship. It may have even spurred Sting on to stardom, but somehow I doubt it.

It certainly didn't do me any good, as our respective paths took dramatically different directions after our days at 'The Old School by the Tyne', as the place was described in a laughable school song.

6 – FRENCH FARCE: *voulez-vous regardez ma poubelle avec moi, ce soir?*

Over the years the beatings continued, though as we grew older they became less frequent. By the time I had my last bottom-bashing in the fourth year, my arse was as hard as a fifty-shilling piss-pot. I had merely asked Fr Boyle if the Devil had a dick. As I had built up a natural immunity, I did not feel any of the blows at all. To this day, I can still crack walnuts with my buttocks if ever called upon to do so, which isn't often, I must admit. Have you ever noticed that unusual people often have unusual names, for example, 'Peregrine Worsthorne' and 'Quentin Crisp' to name but two? The same rule applied to our other first-year French teacher, Douglas Hesp, although by my own logic, I suppose, he should really have been called 'Obadiah Hesp'.

Douglas had two interesting peculiarities. Firstly, considering he was a French teacher, he did not seem to pay too much attention to 'that-there book learning', and he very much did his own thing. That seemed mainly to teach us French words that were virtually useless outside Mr Hesp's lesson. He would try to tell us the French for 'bagpipes', whereas the more basic translations for, say, 'house' or 'friend' were apparently much less important. Sting was unable to remember the French for 'mother' or 'dog', so the chances of him being able to translate 'cauliflower' or 'torpedo' into French were slim, to say the least. As a result Hesp's second forte came into play. Dear old Doug thought it right to punish wrongdoing, for example, not knowing the French for 'shove-halfpenny', by whacking the perpetrator on the backside with what he called 'the slipper'. This was not actually a slipper as most would perceive it but a tennis shoe, or as school personnel insisted on calling them 'indoor shoes'. The powers that were must have thought that we leaden-footed kids would wear away the precious wooden floors with our constant pounding. Perhaps if we had been wearing pit-boots or clogs, they might have had a point. Whatever their logic, indoor shoes were obligatory.

The boy with the biggest feet in the class was always chosen to donate his 'slipper' which would be used to administer swift retribution. Sting was captain of the warmed-arse team. He had more thrashings than Salman Rushdie has had looks out of the window. Bad luck for Sting but it meant bad luck for me as well on occasions.

Being very short-sighted, I sat in one of the front desks in order to be able to read things on the blackboard with something approaching clarity. However, when Hesp was meting out his own individual style of punishment, the one place you did not want to be was in the front row. The ritual posterior-pummelling affected me in a way more horrible than could be imagined. I quite literally felt (and smelled) every blow because Spud Murphy, the donor of the unfeasibly large slipper, had particularly sweaty feet. When Hesp brought down the slipper on Sting's arse, the disgusting fluid that had gathered in the oversized shoes sprayed out with nauseating accuracy all over my desk and, worse, over me on the odd occasion.

'Slipper, Sumner laddie' was an overused phrase that summer. Sting and I would both squirm when Hesp shouted it out. There seemed to be nothing we could do about it. Sting was incapable of learning obscure French words. All Sting could come up with was the idea that, if no one wore 'indoor shoes', Hesp would have nothing to belt us with. Sting duly put a scrap of notepaper in the school suggestion box, advising the authorities to ban the 'slipper' and recommend that everyone wrap rags around their feet instead. The advantages were obvious. No damage would be done to the floors, and there was the added bonus that they'd receive a good polish into the bargain. Surprisingly, the idea was rejected, but at least Sting was trying.

'Rag Doll', the Four Seasons' hit, became our theme song during the autumn of 1964. And we suffered only the odd slippering that term and had some luck because Hesp took to using his own individual slipper – not one he wore, of course, because staff were not required to wear 'indoor shoes'. I believe they had special dispensation from the Pope on the matter. The mercy was that Hesp's own slipper was dry. He used to carry it around with him at all times. Sting said he should have had it in a holster, his hand forever hovering over it like a gunslinger. At the end of that term, I could translate 'My nanny's grasshopper was sick in my chiropodist's bassoon', no bother, but I was stuck on 'My father and brother live in a house'.

Strangely enough, despite his quirks, we kids liked Hesp. He had a certain elan and a warped sense of humour that appealed to most of us. Soon afterwards, Hesp left the school, with the intention no doubt of going and bamboozling some other unsuspecting schoolboys in some other city, filling their heads with French bullshit. Talking of 'shit', I still remember the French for that is 'merde'. Thanks for that at least, Douglas.

7 – THE UNSPEAKABLE IN PURSUIT OF THE UNEDUCATED

Still in our first year, we had a new form master called Mr Brannigan. He was a wiry little man with black greased-back hair. He must have been about 26 years old at the time and had a thick Ashington accent. This is a mining town north of Newcastle and even we Geordies often could not understand what he was saying. After our first lesson with him, the class concluded unanimously that he was an arsehole. As he chattered away at fifty to the dozen, scribbling illegible symbols on the blackboard, the only thing I could make out was '='.

'Any questions?' he asked.

Only my pal Bob Taylor had the nerve to say, 'I don't know about the rest of the class, sir, but I haven't got the foggiest idea what this stuff means. Could you repeat it please a little more slowly?'

Brannigan hurtled to where Bob sat, glared at him and

said, 'Aal reet, pal,' then raced back to the board and, if anything, started scrawling even faster. 'There,' he concluded, 'easy-peezy.' Happy with his handiwork he continued on his merry way. The lesson came to an end with the massed ranks of class 1P none the wiser. Brannigan marched off, leaving us with six similar problems for homework. As Brannigan left, Sting loudly sang 'You're No Good', ably copying the Swinging Blue Jeans' rendition of their Top 10 hit. Peter Kirkley, the only lad in the class who was genuinely any good at maths, had no trouble with the exercise and answered the questions expertly – we all copied his work.

Brannigan seemed to have at least one of the qualities required for a post at the school. He knew his subject well but was unable or unwilling to convey it to his class. He didn't have the 'slipper, laddie' mentality of Hesp, preferring the vicious knuckle to the temple or a short prod to the ribs. We survived, however, as an uneasy truce existed between us. Brannigan would stand in front of the class scratching away at the board, while we sat in a comatose state looking aimlessly ahead. When he had finished, Peter Kirkley would show us what the hell he was on about. The school should have been paying Brannigan's wages to Kirkley.

It was the end of the Christmas term when the truce was broken in spectacular fashion. One of the duties of the form master was to supervise the cramming together of our desks into the middle of the classroom on the last day. The action left a wide space around the outside of the room, like a mini running track. We had completed our task and were awaiting our freedom, signalled by the sound of the school-bell. It rang out and the class surged forward en masse in an attempt to gain early release. The sooner we got away from this bloke, the better.

As we stampeded towards the door led by the fleet-footed Sting, Brannigan, showing an electric turn of pace himself, reached it first and screamed, 'Get back! You can go when I say you can go.'

But he had badly underestimated the pupils' resolve. It was the last day of term and we couldn't give a shit. Sting was only inches away from him and he implored, 'Oh, come on, sir, let us go.'

Brannigan was incensed. 'Back,' he wailed. Badly in need of a whip and a chair, he stood alone. Since he had neither, the pack inched forward. Sting and Brannigan would have been face to face if Sting had not been three inches taller.

Looking Sting squarely in the chin, Brannigan suddenly appeared to lurch forward. With the ringleader out of the way, he could then start on the rest of us. Sting swayed backwards, a manoeuvre which was to prove useful in later years when mortal-drunk. The florid pedagogue tried again to apprehend the smirking youth and again he failed. Sting, thinking that another attempt by the furious Mr B was imminent, took off around the outside of the classroom. Brannigan went after him in hot pursuit.

Young Sting could really shift, so the prey remained a

couple of yards in front of the irate hunter, until the callow youth met up with the rest of the class gathered at the classroom door. One circuit complete, he tried to make the door but was held up through sheer weight of numbers. So he set off on another lap. Brannigan followed. This time, for no apparent reason, the rest of the pupils, led by Bob Taylor, took up the chase. Brannigan chased Sting and everyone else chased Brannigan. Around and around went this insane throng until it was one solid thread encircling the outer limits of the classroom.

Brannigan by now appeared lost somewhere in the middle of this cheering morass of lunatics. The room now resembled the chariot-race scene in *Ben Hur*. This bizarre party game continued for what seemed like a dozen laps, until some genius had the foresight to open the classroom door and the ribbon of racing humanity rushed outside. Remarkably, everyone made it apart from the exhausted and humiliated Brannigan. We set off for home exhilarated by a great victory.

The class sang out Petula Clark's chart-topper 'Downtown'. Sting, not of that musical persuasion, tunelessly whistled the Beatles number 'I Feel Fine', capturing the mood perfectly.

Some years later, Peter Kennedy, another Maths teacher and a good one at that, who sadly died prematurely, told me that he had witnessed the whole ridiculous charade from an adjacent classroom. I asked him why he had not intervened. He told me he had never had any intention of doing so. He said he had never seen anything like it in all his years at the school. 'Better than any Christmas pantomime,' he reckoned. I told him that we were happy to have been of service and I was sad not to be able to repeat the performance because Brannigan left the school before we were given the chance. I think he joined a monastery.

8 – SPUD TAKES ON THE BOSS

The Reverend Canon Martin Cassidy was headmaster of St Cuthbert's during the years we were pupils at the school. He was not just feared and respected by the boys, but by the staff as well. He had the most amazing aura of power and authority about him. No master or pupil ever sought to cross his path. Just short of six feet tall, he always wore the same garb, a long black cassock which reached down to his feet like the other priests, but his had a distinguishing red trim and was finished with red cloth buttons. Even from hundreds of yards away, he was immediately recognisable.

His features were daunting, too. Bald except for a little grey hair, he was a man in his mid-60s with a severe countenance, his face chiselled like a marble mausoleum. Slight stubble on his chin made him look all the more menacing and sinister. He would always promenade the old hall before morning assembly, ambling ever so slowly up and down. Only boys with total confidence in their appearance or complete idiots ever came within hailing distance of him.

April 4th 1965 was a date in the life of the junior Sting that he wouldn't forget in a hurry. Late for the start of the school day as usual, Sting sprinted into the old hall oblivious to the boss's presence. Without looking up, he ploughed into the gaffer at full pace, nearly decking him. If I had not known differently, I would have sworn it was deliberate. He almost sent him flying. The boss glared at Sting like he was a packet of condoms found on a first-year. Not a pretty sight.

'I'm so sorry, Reverend Father, I didn't see you, I'm afraid,' the rampaging lad managed to splutter.

He had given the old man a shoulder-charge which could have felled a bull. It was a tribute to the gaffer's physical strength that he didn't go down.

'You idiotic young fool, you could have killed me,' the boss growled, slightly exaggerating the collision.

As word spread like wildfire that the head had only just survived an attempt on his life, the hall began to fill up with ghouls who only seconds earlier would not have dared to go anywhere near the scene. *Schadenfreude*, I think the Germans call it.

Poor little Sting's apology fell on deaf ears. 'Go to my study after assembly, you careless buffoon,' the head commanded him.

I sang the Moody Blues' No 1 hit 'Go Now', as Sting forlornly trooped off to the boss's study after assembly. He resembled a baby seal which was about to be clubbed as he listened to the words I was singing. The years of avoiding the big cheese were now over for the previously vigilant Sting. It was not so much the accident itself that was so damaging as the fact that he would now be remembered by the boss as a known troublemaker: his name and face would be committed to the head's memory.

Earlier, I had tried to comfort my pal with the notion that the boss would see the collision purely as an accident and that, after a warning never to run in the school building again, everything would be hunky-dory. Sting did not believe my words, and neither did I. In the study the boss lambasted Sting. He got out Sting's academic records, presumably to show him what an idiot he was, though by the age of 15 he already knew that. The boss called him 'insolently indolent', tore him off a strip and sent him out with a flea in his ear. When I saw him later, he was still shaking. He asked me what 'insolently indolent' meant. I very reasonably informed him that, if he did not know, then that was exactly what he was. Sting nodded in agreement. Whatever it meant, I wasn't slow to use the expression in future about people I didn't like. It hasn't done me any harm.

If Sting's untimely clash with the boss was a disaster for him, I was to have a similarly bleak encounter. It was March 1966 and I was quietly singing to myself 'The Sun Ain't Gonna Shine Anymore', the brilliant new No 1 smash for the Walker Brothers. The lyrics were to prove prophetic. I had completed my Geography homework where it was supposed to be done – at home. Unluckily for me, I was comparing one of my diagrams with that of a good friend of mine, Derek Hornsby. I thought his looked better than mine so I quickly copied it, showing a marked lack of judgement the appeals court would be proud of.

As I finished the minor adjustment to my homework with head down, I became aware of an eerie silence which had descended on the class. I looked up to see the most terrifying sight on earth: a row of red cloth buttons. This vision was more than enough for the muscles controlling my bladder to flee screaming from the room. The shock left me with a damp crotch, which, I am ashamed to admit, was the result of sheer terror. I managed to control my limbs but I could not speak.

The boss man glared at me with controlled malevolence. He lifted my book, along with that of the unfortunate Master Hornsby, putting them both under his arm and requested, quite politely I thought, that Derek and I should pay him a little visit after assembly. I told Derek not to worry as I would take all the blame, though he was not totally pacified. In the event, I managed to convince the head that I had taken Derek's book without his knowledge, a very silly thing to have done.

In the study, I got the same sort of treatment as Sting had been dished out previously. I don't think he called me 'insolent' or 'indolent' or a combination of both, but I was in his room much longer than I had hoped to be and I remember sobbing under his constant barrage. At least I didn't wee all over his floor as seemed possible when I first entered his study.

In fact, my punishment was surprisingly light. I was banished from the classroom before morning assembly when I had been expecting a cordial invitation to Fr Walsh's office. Not to be outdone in the name-calling stakes, I told Sting that the boss had called me 'indolently truculent'. He was well impressed.

There were certain pupils – insane ones, I thought – who appeared to have no fear of the boss. They were few and far between but one of them was in our form. 'Spud' Murphy, he of the incredibly large feet, was from a middle-class background, came from Gosforth and talked 'posh'. I always thought he was a bit dim but, if he was, he was also fearless, with skin as thick as Fr Walsh's whacking book. Not long after my visit to the boss when I had only just stopped cowering, we got a surprise in class when the boss suddenly turned up unannounced. I immediately convinced myself he was there to get me; I turned white and felt faint. I looked around to see almost the whole class doing likewise.

It was April 1966 and the Spencer Davis Group were wowing us with their hit 'Somebody Help Me', but daft lads like 'Spud' Murphy never asked for help. They thought they were indestructible. It was so unusual for the boss to appear in class that we were all convinced he was there to drag us to his study for a 'near-death' experience. We were all wrong.

Our Maths master, Bill Mastaglio, was overseeing the class when the Reverend Canon sauntered in. We all stood up at once as a sign of respect for our hallowed visitor. He managed to put us quickly at our ease by calmly announcing, 'Sit down, boys, please,' nice as pie. He quietly continued, 'You will be aware that the school notice board informs you that this form will take the second sitting for lunch this week.' He looked around to see a mass of nodding heads and would have heard many a 'Yes, Father' coming his way.

'There is an error in that instruction. This form will take first sitting for lunch, today and for the foreseeable future. Any problems?' This was a fairly simple piece of information, concisely conveyed – what could be simpler? We were on first lunches, not second.

Why the headmaster was wandering round the school with this piece of trivia was puzzling. The school cat could just about have carried out this simple mission for him. He could have had nothing else to do that morning, I reckoned. But, if the class thought that no one was going to have a problem with this information, they were figuring without the eccentric 'Spud'. As no one had answered his question, the boss was just about to leave when a madman entered the fray.

Spud cleared his throat, with a bark that shook the assembly. 'Aaargh, you have made a mistake, Father,' Spud piped up.

'Christ, this must be important,' I mused as Spud caught the boss's attention.

'You said, did you not, Father, that this form will take "first sitting" for lunch today?' Spud announced, stating the bleeding obvious. Spud blundered on. 'I think you will find that we are actually on second sitting for lunch today.'

A murmur quietly circumnavigated the room. Bill Mastaglio's eyes appeared to be bulging out of their sockets in muted horror as Spud appeared to question the boss's infallibility. The boy was clearly demented. The mesmerised class eagerly awaited the head's reply. Had Spud used his crackpot reasoning to convince himself that the school notice board had more authority than the headmaster did? It sure looked that way. Poor Spud had lost his marbles. The portcullis was up but the castle was empty.

Fr Cassidy finally answered with chilling calm. 'No, son, it is you who is mistaken. As I have already said, this form will take first sitting. Not as the notice board says, but as *I* say. Is that clear?'

Spud had apparently escaped without penalty, despite his crazy logic. Or so we all thought. Spud, plainly bent on suicide, could not be pacified and would not be denied. 'I'm sorry, Father, but it is most definitely you who is in the wrong here. This is "3P", you know? We're on seconds today. It's there on the notice board, if you would only take a look.'

We all looked at each other in total disbelief. Mastaglio

had turned blue. Gasps of incredulity had met Spud's admonishment to the boss. His sheer idiocy was sure to get him thrown out of the school if he kept this up. Insolent indolence, if ever I saw it. The boss, incredibly, was still serene, making a malevolent joke that only the boy Murphy failed to recognise. 'What is your name, son?' the boss kindly asked.

'Murphy, Father,' the daft kid replied, almost smiling.

'Well, Murphy, as you know so much about it,' the canon said, bristling with derision, 'you might as well take over and tell the class which sitting you all will take for lunch today. As I am only the Headmaster and I obviously do not know what I am talking about, please come out to the front of the class and give them the news because you are now in charge.'

Sting, sitting in the desk behind Murphy, whispered, 'Don't move a friggin' muscle, Spud.'

It was good advice but Spud had his engine running and he rapidly took up the offer. The room was hushed – Bill Mastaglio had apparently fainted – as Spud strode purposefully from his desk, now the school's new supremo. I turned and looked at Sting, his head in his hands, as the rest of us sat there agog with anticipation. At the front of the class, Spud beamed from ear to ear and shouted, 'Father Cassidy has, quite wrongly, informed us we will be on first sitting for lunch this week. We are in fact...'

But he didn't get to finish his sentence. The boss, who had been listening with arms folded, suddenly lost patience and lunged at Murphy, grabbing him by the ear and leading him out of the classroom. He was taking him up to his study for what we all assumed would be the mother and father of all thrashings.

At break-time Spud was amazingly unrepentant. He claimed that he received little more than a ticking-off. Not only that, but he still insisted that he was right and the boss was wrong. The upshot was that Spud and two lunatic followers missed their lunches that day. They had gone to second sittings. I remember thinking at the time – and advising Sting accordingly – that it was best to have nothing whatsoever to do with Spud Murphy. He was a very dangerous lad to know.

9 – FOOT-IN-MOUTH DISEASE

Considering that the boss was such a commanding figure who was feared and revered by all – except Murphy, of course – he had an incredible knack of making a fool of himself. Normally this happened at pre-school assembly, when he managed to say the daftest things. While giving his usual post-prayers pep talk to all the wasters in the school, and there were many, someone could be heard muttering as the boss rambled on. He stopped abruptly, indignantly announcing, 'Every time I open my mouth, some fool speaks!' Some of the tough fifth-years sniggered, though the thick ones did not see the joke. Other clever-dick sixth-years nodded sagely in mock appreciation. Most just bit their lips, while a good many were simply not listening.

Perhaps, though, his finest gaffe came when some hooligans kept carving their desks with penknives.

Complaining to the school that a large sum of cash had to be found to replace the disfigured desks, he bellowed at us, 'The school cannot afford the money that needs to be spent on replacement desks. *Do you think wood grows on trees?*' Well, actually… yes, we did, boss.

To put it mildly, the head was not an amusing or witty person and assembly in the mornings was by no means laugh-a-minute knockabout entertainment. Only once can I recall the boss attempting levity. Almost inevitably, it all ended in tears. I don't remember what he actually said but everyone was so surprised that his remarks were intended as humour that laughter swept the hall and grew to a crescendo. As near-hysteria broke out, kids fell about helpless. 'All right, all right, it wasn't that funny. Control yourselves,' scolded the boss.

Everyone ceased the histrionics, except one smarmy sixth-year who continued guffawing, now clearly taking the piss. 'Hee, hee, haw, haw, oh my aching sides,' he wailed.

The boss heard his voice and, noticing it was coming from the back of the hall, the sixth-form domain, he issued a challenge: 'Is someone trying to take a rise out of me?' (Priests aren't allowed to say 'the piss'.)

I thought, Come on, who is it? Own up and we will have it out, here and now.

No one answered.

The boss's whole demeanour changed. He went on, 'Ah, I see, a coward hiding at the back of the hall. Come on, I'll take you on any time.'

It sounded more like a threat from one first-year to another. Did he seriously intend to give the smirking teenager his go? The head was obviously spoiling for a fight. In my mind I had the image of the head and a strapping sixer wading into each other behind the bike-sheds, with Fr Walsh holding the warlike priest's cassock and howling, 'Go on, Reverend Father, rip the fucker's head off.' I smiled to myself. Luckily for the boss, the piss-taker did not take up his offer of a punch-up, letting down the whole school in the process. Jim Reeves's 'Distant Drums' had recently been a big hit, though not with me or Sting, but Sting could just be heard singing it and pointing to the guilty sixth-former who had robbed us all of a rumble in the refectory.

Assembly was always tedious but two other memorable incidents stand out. In August 1966, Fr Walsh took a day's sick leave. At the end of assembly, he used to conduct matters like a traffic policeman. All the forms stood in long lines waiting for his instructions. Only Fr Walsh among the staff knew where all the classes were meant to go. As neatly orchestrated lines of kids marched off in every direction, it used to resemble a scene from the Royal Tournament. Forms often came within a whisker of colliding with one another... that was until Fr Walsh had his day off.

Even though the school could have cleared the hall, blindfold, without any instructions in two minutes flat, we stood there silently daring the boss to make a mistake. For example, we were hoping he would order a form forward when it should have about-turned. It was only seconds before we were granted our wish. It was our form, the glorious 3P, who were given the erroneous instruction to head straight on when we should have turned around. Not a single boy stopped or even hesitated, before plunging headlong into 2P, going the same way. The boss gaped in horror but again inadvertently gave another misleading instruction and the same thing happened.

Two more classes crashed into each other with gay abandon. The same scenario was repeated all over the hall until the place was in a state of total disarray. Haphazard juvenile delinquency reigned. Even the sixth-form, not known for their japes, joined in the fun. Some kids adopted a sleepwalking pose, arms outstretched, while Sting hummed 'Strangers in the Night' to himself. At first, the head shouted counter-instructions, but he soon gave up and settled for quitting the scene. He pushed his way past the interwoven hordes of staggering schoolboys as if this had nothing to do with him. Thank God, Fr Walsh will be back on the morrow, he must have thought.

The other act of high drama was almost as chaotic, though not as many people were affected. It was almost a year later, in June 1967, when pandemonium broke out again due to one boy's spectacular performance at assembly. In the summer months, some stupid git would always faint in the stifling heat. There was nothing unusual in that. The culprit would often be seen swaying at first, allowing fellow pupils to catch him or, more often than not, move smartly out of his way. So when in assembly one morning we noticed a body gently moving from side to side, we thought, Here we go again.

The lad standing in the next form-line to Sting and mine was, however, no fainter. Spewing his guts up turned out to be his speciality. Suddenly he gave out a terrifying, animal-like roar. Then he arched his back, jerked violently forward and gave an expert impression of a fire hydrant, expelling his liquefied breakfast from his gaping mouth at great speed. From where Sting and I were standing, it was a glorious sight. But, if you were positioned just in front of the sick kid, it couldn't have been nearly as amusing.

In fact, he managed to cover a dozen or so schoolmates with his vile eruption. One question begged to be answered: why had he eaten several cans of cream of vegetable soup for his morning repast? Well, that was judging by the amazing explosion of copious amounts of coloured liquid. I had seen people being sick before, and many since, but this lad was in a class of his own. The volume and distance involved would be a joy to anyone interested in 'Vomitobatics'. But not everyone was as impressed as I was, certainly not those who were covered in the stuff. Some came out in sympathy with the lad and promptly jettisoned their own breakfasts over bystanders.

I noticed that no one else had consumed such vast quantities of soup for their morning meal. It appeared that the rest had contented themselves with the traditional diced carrots and tomato skins. The combination of gallons of sick, rubber-soled pumps and a highly polished wooden floor, together with a mass exodus from the epicentre of the explosions, proved a highly successful recipe for much activity of the 'falling-on-your-arse' variety. At least thirty people ended up so indisposed. The scene came straight out of a Tom Sharpe novel. Sting and I were models of compassion. We laughed until we were sick... well, not quite. Sting sang Procol Harem's chart-topper 'Whiter Shade of Pale', though nobody quite turned cartwheels in the end.

The lad responsible for this magnificent spectacle was called Joe McLean, someone Sting knew better than I did. He sometimes got a game for the school football team. After that day, he was looked upon with great respect and given the epithet 'Spewer' McLean. I don't know where you are these days, 'Spewer', old son, but I remember that summer day and the ructions you caused when shouting for 'Hughie' and 'Ralph'. I hope you eat a more conventional breakfast these days, Joe.

Whatever anyone thought of the boss, it could not be denied that he did his level best for the school. He often referred to the place as 'My School' and he meant it. When he died some time after our school days, it was a much poorer place for his passing. Every 'old boy' should have mourned his death. After all, he spent almost his entire adult life trying to make our lives better. If he failed – as in many cases – it was our own fault, not his. He would have died for St Cuthbert's and everyone knew that. The school would never see his like again.

10 – STING, PRIESTS AND THE ANTICHRIST

I knew that priests ran the school long before I ever attended. Fr Walsh, Fr Duffy, Fr Daley, Fr Tweedy, Fr Boyle and Fr Craven all lent their support to the Headmaster, the Reverend Canon Martin Cassidy. Some we liked and some we didn't like.

The youngest was Fr Duffy, our first-year master. He was a new boy with a pale complexion and jet-black hair, worn short of course in a kind of fringe that he might have thought modern-looking. Everyone liked 'Pop Duff'. He was a nice man and he understood many of the problems associated with young boys at a new school, even if there was not that much he could do about some spotty fifth-year punching you in the nose because you accidentally splashed his shoes when having a 'wee' in the urinals. I don't know how long 'Pop Duff' spent at St Cuthbert's; I just got the impression he would rather have been somewhere else.

Fr Tweedy was a more down-to-earth type. Fortyish, tall and stockily built with more hair than the other priests, he wore thick, thick spectacles – the type you need to have brilliant eyesight to be able to see out of. He ended up in prison – no, not for any crime, but as the Chaplain at Durham Jail. His experience in dealing with homicidal maniacs, perverts, thieves and fraudsters must have been invaluable when he left the school for prison service.

Fr Daley was more like you expected a priest to look. He was small, had greying hair and was about sixty years old. Frail-looking and miserably benign, he never actually taught either Sting or me but I always thought him to be a bit of a pain in the arse. He once umpired a house cricket match and gave me out LBW to a ball that would have knocked second slip's teeth out. He seemed to do sod-all at school and he spoke in a whisper, a trait I have never liked – except in the confessional box.

My abiding memory of Fr Daley came when the head, Canon Cassidy, died. Sting and I attended the funeral. To my amazement, Fr Daley was being touted as favourite to take on the mantle of new headmaster. At the time, I was in the habit of taking bets on just about anything and I opened a book on who would get the job. Standing next to me, Sting was visibly moved and whispered, 'Twenty quid on Fr Walsh for the headship.' The bet was struck and a few days later Sting drew his winnings when Fr Walsh was installed as the new headmaster. I learned a valuable lesson: never be caught unawares where betting is concerned. I never got caught like that again; instead I got caught in dozens of other ways.

Fr Boyle was universally known as 'Elyob' – the school mania for spelling names backwards gave Sting his original nickname of 'Nodrog' or 'Noddy', as he was called for some time. Fr Boyle was thin but quite wiry-looking, 60-ish, bald and apparently inoffensive. He came over as something of an intellectual, who fancied himself as a new Gerald Manley Hopkins. That could have been because his brother was a well-known author, who wrote a book outing double agents in MI6 which caused quite a stir a few years later.

My old friend Michael Walsh had told me that Elyob had a terrible temper but I never believed it. It was like being told that you must not rile Santa Claus because he has another side to him. It was all a bit hard to swallow but Michael turned out to be right. I found that out to my cost in a Religious Education lesson. Fr Boyle asked why Lazarus had not been buried in a grave. I answered in flamboyant style, 'Was it because he was not dead, Father?' It wasn't the wittiest retort I have ever given but I did not expect him to round on me in the way he did, almost frothing at the mouth in fury. But he calmed down as quickly as he had flared up and that was that.

Fr Craven was a Chief Superintendent in the Cuthbert's police. Mid-30s, short and stocky, he had wire-wool-type hair, black and brushed back. He also had a square face, permanent five o'clock shadow and absolutely enormous lips. He could have given the kiss of life to Jaws. He was known to everyone as 'Kipper Lips'.

He seemed to spend an awful lot of time mooching around classes at break-times looking for scraps of rubbish invisible to everyone but him. He would order you to pick up things that had nothing whatsoever to do with you. He only taught us RE very briefly in our third year and I recall one day he told us that he had been to the cinema, the 'Stoll', in Newcastle and had been filled with revulsion after seeing a sexy scene. He immediately stormed in to the manager's office and demanded his money back.

Fr Craven left the priesthood a few years later for the love of a good woman. He's still married with a grown-up family. Well done, that man!

The priest we most came into contact with, unluckily for us, was Fr Walsh, punishment master and Deputy Head. Already described on these pages, he was all over the place like the smell of school dinners.

Sting was almost on personal terms with Fr Walsh by the time we left. His visits were on such a regular basis he should have asked for a season ticket, or even discount. Sting was simply unable or unwilling to conform to the school regime. His schoolwork was not that bad. If it had been, he would have gone the way of many terminal slackers before him – he would have been asked to leave.

His indiscretions were minor ones. For example, he would not wear the correct school uniform. He would wear flares instead of the regulation grey slacks. He would wear a mauve sweater instead of grey. And almost every day he would be late for school. Most days he would dawdle in at his own pace to be met by the uncompromising figure of Fr Craven – sometimes the time would be approaching ten o'clock. Sting gave the impression that he had a part-time job. He always had a good excuse though. But if the number of teeth he reportedly had had extracted at the dentist's had been accurate, he would have looked like 'Old Mother Riley'.

The problem that most often caused Sting to have run-ins with the hierarchy was his hair. Back then it was his pride and joy, even if it has so sadly let him down in recent years. In those days, if not now, the lad was obsessed with his tonsorial elegance. His ambition was beautifully simple: he intended to have the trendiest hairstyle in the school – not all that difficult a task, I thought.

Almost every kid in the school sported a horrendous haircut. They littered the place. Boys looked like they had had their heads shaved and their bald pates daubed with a strong glue, then rammed into a bucket of hair swept up from the barber's floor. Not the boy Sting, however! He wanted to look as though Vidal Sassoon had spent all morning preparing him for the rigours of the school day ahead. In our senior years when long hair was more popular, it became a major problem for our dedicated follower of fashion.

St Cuthbert's schoolboys were always required to wear their hair as short as was feasibly possible, no matter what fashion dictated. Sting had other ideas. To be perceived by all as a cool dude, Sting decided that he must have at least shoulder-length locks. So he grew his hair 'Down the West Road', as the boss once drolly described the style.

Sting would spend all day trying to avoid walking into any of the St Cuthbert's hair police, namely any of the priests or busybody Geography master, 'Noddy' Lunn. It was Mission Impossible. They pounced on Sting quicker than a cheetah wearing roller-skates could catch a wart hog with four wooden legs. His refusal to get his hair cut was to lead to many visits to Fr Walsh and his favourite piece of wood.

Years later, Sting's admission in tabloid rags that he endured some 48 canings in one term was a little bit over the top. If that had been true, his arse would have looked like an aerial photograph of Clapham Junction! Nevertheless, I know of no one who got more hidings than Sting, though a lad called Les Mutrie must have run him close.

In March 1967, tired of the regular whackings, Sting decided to do something about his hair problem. Getting it cut would have been the most sensible response but Sting was too ingenious to settle for such craven action. To keep the trimming scissors at bay, the insolently indolent junior milkman preferred to give the impression that his tresses had already been shorn by inserting a series of hairpins into the back of his flowing locks. This stopped his hair from reaching his collar. Only by standing an inch away from his neck, could you make out the six small pieces of metal that kept him from yet another arse-bending.

Each morning on the bus to school, I would dutifully make sure everything was in place. But, like all good wheezes, it eventually came unstuck. At school he had been wearing his hair like this for several weeks. When released, it flopped six inches past his collar. He looked like an Apache who had murdered a schoolboy on a wagon train, stolen his school blazer and now the renegade wore it proudly as a trophy. At school, he was a tidy, well-groomed young man. At four o'clock, he became a juvenile delinquent, his hair cascading down his back.

I fell into the habit of singing Engelbert Humperdinck's 'Release Me' as we went through the gates at the end of the school day, just as Sting let go his rippling mane.

It all went terribly wrong when Sting's hair was so long that, even with the clips holding it firm, it still stretched down past collar length, the benchmark for the St Cuthbert's hair-commissioners. Sting and I were standing in the old hall prior to morning assembly when Walshy approached stealthily like a giant black spider. Before we had the chance to leg it, the priest had fallen upon Sting. 'Get your hair cut and soon, mister!' he demanded, which in itself was not the end of the world. But his simultaneous actions were to prove decisive. As the priest spoke, he also flicked at the back of Sting's head to indicate the illegal length of his hair, dislodging the pins holding it in place. Sting's precious locks fell from their bonds, flowing halfway down his back. In an instant, he became a Troll, a wild thing.

Fr Walsh staggered back, as if confronted by the Antichrist. He mumbled something inaudible, waving vaguely in our direction before turning his back and hurrying away, presumably to find the comfort of the other clergy. On reflection, I just think that Sting had shocked him rigid with his incredible appearance. 'Thought we were in trouble for a minute there' was all I could get from Sting. The Wild Man of Borneo then politely asked me to replace the fallen pins, which I did. His tresses back intact, Sting managed to keep up the act until fashion demanded his hair be lopped off. At least by then he had lost one reason for his regular visits for the cane but he was still going to have to work on the other 27...

11 – THE MAN WHO SHOT KENNEDY

November 1963: Friday night was spent like all other Friday nights – Mam was at the Bingo, Dad and I were watching TV together. At 7.00pm, it was time for *Take Your Pick* 'with your quiz inquisitor', Michael Miles. 'Take the money' or 'Open the box' we would shout at the screen, fully believing that the contestants could hear us and were influenced by our encouragement. Then suddenly there was an announcement: 'We interrupt this programme for a news flash. The President of the United States, John F Kennedy, has been shot in Dallas, Texas. His condition is described as serious. More news later, meanwhile back to *Take Your Pick*.'

My dad and I looked at each other and grimaced. Kennedy had seemed to be a good man and a fine president. We were hoping that he would be OK, but a few minutes later the newsreader announced the death of the most powerful figure on earth. Although he was an American, albeit with strong ties across the Atlantic, the impact of his death was enormous. The old adage that everyone can remember where he or she was when Kennedy died was certainly true for me, even if the circumstances were mundane in the extreme.

Although it was a couple of days later, discussion on the way to school still centred on the awful event in Dallas. The first person I met on the bus was the blond lad with the gloomy expression, young Sumner. 'What do you think of the assassination of the president?' I asked, knowing that the lad kept in touch with world events, though admittedly he could hardly have missed this one.

He sat there granite-faced, more like a member of the government than a schoolboy. 'Tragic, horrific, terrible. Such a waste of life. I couldn't believe it,' he said in a deep melancholy. 'I was listening to some music at the time, "I Wanna Be Your Man", you know, by the Rolling Stones.' He was clearly appalled at the ignorance that my blank expression betrayed.

'I was watching *Take Your Pick* on the telly. Dad and me always watch it,' I innocently remarked, not prepared for the backlash to come.

'Christ, no! Not bloody *Take Your Pick*. I can't stand that shite!' he spat back. 'I thought you had more wit than to watch some crappy quiz show.'

I reasoned to myself that he might have been right about the president's tragic death but I'd be buggered if I would let him get away with his condemnation of my favourite quiz. 'What's wrong with *Take Your Pick*, you big girl?' I replied.

In an instant one of the most dramatic nights in history was forgotten as we argued about the merits of a TV programme.

'Look, I told you it's a pile of doo-doo,' he insisted.

'Piss off, is it?' I ranted.

'Oh, fuck off,' Sumner shouted, getting off the bus.

I grunted and caught up with him, though we walked through the school gates in silence. The first lad we saw that we knew was Frank Corr. Thinking that Frank would be a sure-fire *Take Your Pick* fan, I ploughed in. 'All right, Frankie, were you watching *Take Your Pick* when Kennedy bought it?'

Frank Corr was one of those kids you vividly remember from your school days – there's someone like him in everyone's class. A little fat lad with an ill-fitting uniform, he wore short trousers until he was 16. Throughout history, his haircut has never been in fashion. Beneath it shone a perpetually smiling face in the Cheshire Cat mould, set off by wire-rimmed specs that continually ran down his nose and needed replacing every five seconds.

He was a smashing little lad, daft as a brush, and he had a bit of an unusual dad, too. He was a bookmaker, who unfortunately stood out from the crowd as he only had one arm. He once made the local press when, much to Frank's chagrin, he was cruelly described as 'a one-armed bandit'. Frank must have had a slightly unusual home life; apparently he had spent the entire weekend in his room doing his homework. Without a word from the outside, he was possibly the only person in the western world who was unaware of the cataclysmic events in the USA.

'What's *Take Your Pick*?' Frank asked as Sting grinned widely.

'Terrible news about Kennedy, eh, Frank?' Sting went on.

Frank Corr looked at us decidedly puzzled. The only Kennedy who meant anything to Frank was Peter Kennedy, the Maths master, a much-liked figure at the school. 'Why, what's happened to Kennedy?' asked Frank in his ignorance.

'*He's dead*, man. Where the hell have you been hiding?' Sting asked.

'No one's told me, I've been working this weekend, you know, homework,' Frank lamented. 'Heart attack, was it?'

'Friggin' heart attack! Why, man, he was shot,' I gasped, as Sting bit his lip.

'Shot, eh? Bloody hell. Was it in the papers?' Frank asked.

'Of course it was in the papers and the TV almost all the time. Are you sure your dad didn't lock you in a cupboard?' Sting mocked.

'I've been busy, that's all. Does anyone know who did it?' Frank enquired.

'They have already arrested someone for the murder,

Lee Harvey Oswald they call him,' I replied, well genned-up on the subject. No cupboard for me that weekend.

'Lee Harvey Oswald, eh?' Frank mused. 'Is he a schoolkid?'

Sting and I looked at each other in disbelief, not yet realising that daft Frank thought it was our Maths master who had been gunned down. 'Why would a fucking schoolboy shoot Kennedy? You're barmy, Frank!' I admonished but Frank's mind was running riot.

'I think you might be wrong there, lads. I'm sure this Oswald kid is a third-year. Why would he want to shoot Peter Kennedy? Why didn't he shoot that git Noddy Lunn?'

Sting and I now realised that Frank thought that a crazed third-year, Lee Harvey Oswald in fact, had shot dead the revered Maths master for an unknown reason. 'Yeah, you're absolutely right, Frankie. As Kennedy was leaving the school on Friday night, this Oswald kid, hiding in the book depository, shot him three times and killed him.'

'Bloody hell!' Frank exclaimed, rushing off to tell those who didn't already know the terrible news. He found out the real truth only moments later. He must have been too embarrassed to come back and berate us for our story. Neither Frank nor us two ever mentioned the subject again.

12 – INCENSED

Going to a school that was run by priests was turning out to be a disaster for me. I had been quick off the mark with my admission of adultery in the very first term but even that paled into insignificance compared to my next religious blunder.

Inevitably, Sting played a leading role. That summer, the Beatles' 'Help!' was a hit song. It turned out to be appropriate for me. Every Wednesday afternoon, the school attended the ceremony of Benediction in the big main hall. This was an uncomplicated service that was conducted by one of the priests and two altar boys. Sting and I were doing our usual slouch around the school at lunchtime, when Fr Walsh appeared from nowhere, gesturing us towards him. We tried to pretend that we hadn't noticed him and took off like gazelles in the other direction. But he called loudly after us, so with discretion being the better part of valour we stopped to take our medicine.

'Yes, you two. You can assist at Benediction this afternoon,' he commanded, to our great consternation.

As neither of us had been altar boys since primary school, this was a bit of a choker. Our reputation as 'hard lads' could be wrecked. 'But we haven't assisted before, Father,' Sting countered, as usual speaking for me as well – an annoying habit of his, though on this occasion he was forgiven.

'Well, you had better start some time. You will get ten minutes' rehearsal beforehand,' said the priest.

We detested the idea but we completed our run-through without a hitch. We didn't know which of the priests would be officiating at the ceremony. It would make a big difference if it were, say, Fr Daley who we could not stand or, heaven forbid, the boss himself. We were on fairly safe ground there, we thought, as the boss took Benediction only once in a blue moon.

'Excuse me, Father, who will be taking Benediction today?' I asked Pop Duff, who was about to do the rehearsal, hoping it would be him.

'I believe the Headmaster will do the honours today,' he replied to our horror. He might just as well have told us that the 'Moors Murderer', Ian Brady, was coming to tea; we could not have been more distressed. This was turning into a nightmare. 'Which one of you wants to be the Thurifer?' asked the priest. This is the altar assistant, who had the doubtful privilege of swinging the incense-burner, or thurible, as it was called.

'*He does*!' we shouted in unison, pointing at each other. Naturally, I was picked for the job. This consisted of carrying the censer around the altar and generally waving it about. At one point, the priest would kneel before me and I would shake it in his face as an act of purification. Please do not let it be the boss, I prayed. The long chains of the thurible could be difficult to manoeuvre, but, as long as I did not drop it on the ground, I hoped I would manage my task OK.

We donned our rather washed-out red cassocks and white cottas, then we got some great news. The boss had been called away on urgent business, perhaps to exorcise a first-year caught without rosary beads. When we heard, though, that it would be old sourpuss, Fr Daley, who would step in, our hearts sank again. 'Would you put a small piece of charcoal in the thurible please, my son, and put a match to it?' the old duffer asked. I did as he asked. Then he told me to put two small spoonfuls of incense on the burning charcoal. My first mistake! I asked Sting to do this for me as the incense box was right next to him.

While I listened to the priest tell me the right way to do the blessing, the demonic Sting went into action. Whether he misheard me when I told him how many spoonfuls were needed – thinking I had said '36' and not 'two', or when I said 'spoonfuls', he had heard 'shovelfuls' – I don't know. Whatever the reason, instead of a tiny amount going into the burner, there was now a mountainous pile of the stuff waiting to be unleashed on all and sundry.

It seemed that all was going well. Sting and I were performing with commendable aplomb, even if our status as tough guys was being badly compromised because we looked like two beat-up clowns. The incense was pungent but bearable. Virtually the whole school was assembled in the hall for the ceremony. There was a great deal of coughing going on but I was unperturbed. After all, the World Snooker Champion-ships always take place in the bronchial ward of a major hospital if the noises from the audience are anything to go by.

Then came my next mistake. As a result of the increase in the fumes coming from the censer, I closed my eyes. As I wafted my weapon about, eyes tight-shut, the excess incense started to billow out in spectacular fashion. The point in the service had arrived where the priest knelt before me to be blessed with incense. I opened my eyes for the first time in a couple of minutes to see a faint figure in front of me, more keeling than kneeling. Fr Daley lurched forward, fighting for breath. I responded by waving the thurible in his face, as requested. He went a funny colour. There was a cacophony of gasping and coughing now as Sting finally took matters into his own hands. He shouted at me, 'Get the fuck out of here!' I believed this profanity to be a sure-fire reason for immediate excommunication, but I did as he bid or so I thought.

However, instead of leaving the hall by the nearby exit, I was disorientated and marched the wrong way, straight into the massed ranks of suffocating schoolboys. I exacerbated the problem by continuing to waft the thurible about as if it were part of the ceremony. Choking boys implored me to piss off as I approached them. Amid blasphemous disapproval, I found myself at the back of the hall, the acrid smoke finally clearing slightly. I nipped down the backstairs, incense still pouring from the sodding thing. Finally outside the building, I pulled open the thurible and chucked a huge pile of incense on to the grass, stamping on it in a wild frenzy; at the same time I was cursing that useless twat Sting for getting me in another position of religious delirium.

When I gingerly retraced my steps back to the hall, it was empty. The air still reeked of incense and I could see a familiar figure standing by the far exit, the cause of all the pandemonium. I hurtled towards him, cassock flapping, fully intending to thrash him to within an inch of his life. When I got near, I could hear fits of laughter. 'You've got to go and see Fr Daley,' he managed to get out, still laughing all over his face and halfway down his back.

'Never,' I mocked. 'Whatever for?'

'I think it's because you have killed 16 schoolboys and the school cat,' Sting replied, deadpan.

'What do you mean *I've* killed them?' I protested, not wishing to seem bothered that anyone was dead, just that it was not my fault.

'Nah. Nobody is dead, or even queasy. You'll just get a bollocking, that's all,' Sting sympathetically informed me.

'Oh, aye, I'll get a bollocking, all right! What about you, you arse? It was your entire fault. You put a stone of incense in that bloody thing!'

'I don't suppose it had anything to do with you standing eyes closed, wafting it around till people fainted, did it?' he pointed out with some justification.

'Is Fr Daley mad?' I asked.

'*Mad*!' Sting yelped. 'Why man, he's *incensed*!' and he burst into howls of laughter yet again. After a few seconds pause, I joined him.

I trooped off to see Fr Daley, reflecting that it could have been a damned sight worse if the boss had been the recipient of the assault. If that had been the case, once I had got outside I would have kept on walking until I reached the coast and disappeared until the smoke had cleared, to coin a phrase.

I met the recovering Fr Daley in the vestry, where he sat with his dog collar off. 'What you did out there today was a disgrace. An affront to Our Lord. Not to mention that someone could have died out there,' he said. No matter what sort of trouble I managed to get myself into, I was always told that 'someone could have been killed'. Overdramatic or what?

'There was too much incense in the burner, Father. It was an accident. I'm so sorry, Father. It won't happen again.'

Not surprisingly, we were never asked to assist again. There was a rumour sweeping the school that we had planned the whole event. And, though I can't speak for

Sting, I know that I had nothing to do with any such plot, but the new kudos we acquired did us no harm. Our status was intact: we were still loveable rogues.

13 – CHEMICAL OVER-REACTIONS

As the years passed, despite the great disparity in our ability to warble a tune, our friendship was cemented. Somehow, though, we managed to find trouble whatever we did. Bill Hemy was another master who proved the rule: 'unusual name, strange character'. Short, rotund and bald-headed, he would have been in his 60s at the time. He had a kind of puppet-like face, shiny and reddened. After a couple of years with Bill, most of the class thought he was nuts but I preferred to describe him as eccentric. A fairly jovial sort of bloke unlike most of his fellow tutors, he would never be seen dead in a jacket with leather patches on the elbows. Being a Chemistry master, he would have been fully justified in wearing one. Bill always sported a light-coloured suit and seemed to own several different ones, unlike the majority of the staff, who changed their clothes about as often as Rupert the Bear did.

JAMES BERRYMAN

I suppose he tried to teach us his subject but we never took a blind bit of notice. In the end he took the fairly unorthodox step, considering that we spent a lot of our time in the laboratory, of not allowing us to take part in any experiments. This came about as a result of our first serious venture into the practical side of the subject, when no one handed back the instruments we had just used at the end of the lesson. Test tubes, blowpipes, Bunsen burners, all mysteriously disappeared. These items turned up again all over the school in the weirdest places, like inside the hood of a master's duffle coat. Our punishment was that Practical Chemistry went off the agenda for the time being. Sting and I often sat together playing 'Hang Man' or 'Noughts and Crosses' to while away the lesson. At the end of that term we both attained the same exam mark, 14 per cent – joint bottom. There was room for improvement, one might think. At the end of our next term, we again shared the same result, this time 94 per cent. Some improvement!

It was not that we had worked any harder. We were, in fact, still joint bottom; the top mark was 247 per cent due to the fact that we had marked each other's papers and bribery and threats of violence were rife.

Our form, 3P, was described by a History master, Mr Nichols, as being 'outwardly evil, with an undercurrent of surly sarcasm'. High praise indeed, given the level of competition! The class was a formidable foe for any master to tackle. We may have been a rabble but our team spirit was admirable. One day early in 1965, 3P and

Bill Hemy met head on in a battle of wills that entered St Cuthbert's folklore. Bill had gone away from the lab for a minute, leaving us unsupervised. Free of instrumentation, we had nothing to do but gabble to each other at a rate of decibels. This we were doing with gusto.

Bill returned to the lab to be met by a crescendo of nattering. His first call for quiet was largely ignored, mainly because he could not be heard above the hubbub. Instead of trying to shout us down – farting against thunder, you might think – he decided on a more unusual, indeed extreme, remedy. He picked up a large metal clamp-stand and suddenly crashed it down with all his might on to an asbestos worktop. It smashed to pieces, which sounded like the *Ark Royal* was breaking up. His action, dramatic to say the least, had the desired effect – we stopped talking.

'You see, I can make as much noise as you can, can't I?' he said, understating the case. At that precise moment, he was probably making more noise than anyone else on earth. To ensure he was getting his point across, he started on the next worktop and then continued his crusade against asbestos tops with another ferocious assault. Again he smashed the offending piece into fragments.

Sting whispered to me, 'I hope he collects that up and sprinkles it on his cornflakes.'

At first the class had watched in muted appreciation of Bill's efforts to rid the world of asbestos worktops. As it appeared he had only just began his mission, some started to give yells of encouragement. 'Go on, sir, smash the rest up,' I heard someone shout. Bill, totally oblivious to the real world, continued crashing away to increasing cries of support. The class was now making more noise than the moment when Bill had returned, which somewhat defeated his object. The racket rose to a climax of baying and howling. Singing broke out, with The Beatles' 'Yellow Submarine' to the fore. '*We all live in a chemistry lab*,' we chanted.

I was expecting a conga to form at any second. The lab door was suddenly flung open and in marched Spike 'neepazs, tweezas, peenchas' Hughes. He had obviously heard the cacophony of noise and come to investigate. We shut up almost immediately. Bill just kept on hammering away. His clamp-stand was now only a piece of twisted metal. Spike rushed over to him shouting, 'Mr Hemy, Mr Hemy, what seems to be the problem?' as if there was any problem that could be solved by smashing all the worktops in the lab.

Bill stopped his latest attack and stared glassily at Spike before replying calmly, 'Ah, Mr Hughes, I was just showing the boys that I can make more noise than they can.'

Spike surveyed the scene of former worktops and the deformed clamp-stand, then answered just as calmly, 'Yes, I'm sure you can, Mr Hemy, er, very well done!' Bill seemed happy with this commendation and dropped his cudgel to the floor with a loud clank. 'You see, I told you I could,' Bill said quietly to the assembled masses, receiving a few sage nods of assent from the class, who were now completely silent. Spike led Hemy away from the lab, offering him a cup of tea to calm him down. A minute or so earlier, a straitjacket would have been more appropriate. Bill didn't return to class, so we finished it as we had begun it... playing 'Hang Man'.

14 – THE DAY WE SAWED BILL HEMY'S LEG OFF

Bill never explained his bout of insanity that day and thankfully never repeated it. I guess, after years of ridicule, he just flipped. But the elders of 3P were not going to let Bill off scot-free after his venture into the world of paranoia. He had to be punished. It was lucky that it was the soporific Spike Hughes who had intervened in the worktop massacre. If the boss had walked in on the class with us singing and the master going berserk, I shudder to think what might have happened. Was the rack still in use?

A plan was hatched to humiliate Hemy in front of as many people as possible. After a lot of conspiratorial discussion, it was decided that our best chance to fix the mad chemist would be at morning mass. While the upper school was attending mass in the main hall – having their ears assaulted by the boss's incredibly bad singing voice –

the lower school, including our class, had their own mass in the old hall. Bill Hemy played the organ at these masses, usually on a Holy day of obligation.

This organ, it was rumoured, was only ever seen at these ceremonies. Bill brought it from home, apparently strapped to his back. It was St Cuthbert's Day and both the upper and lower schools were assembled for their respective masses. This was to be Retribution Day. Only a chosen few were privy to inside information that something dramatic might occur in the old hall at mass that morning. Sting and I knew that Bill was in for a fright and that it would be simple and spiteful. During mass, while Bill hammered away at the keyboard, his stool would give way under him, putting him on his arse and sending the watching lower school into raptures. A vindictive pupil had sawn through one of the legs of the stool, which would collapse under Bill's weight when he started moving about on it. Any sideways movement would cause it to break, rendering the poor old chemist well and truly pole-axed.

Despite all Bill's nonsense, I quite liked him so I had misgivings about the plan. But with the sabotaged stool now in place, there was nothing I could do. If past form was anything to go by, the collapse of the stool was just a formality; when playing the organ, Bill used to jump about on it with gay abandon. In fact, he would bounce around on it so much that he was always left exhausted after the performance. When he finally rose to his feet after mass, he used to look like he had just finished wrestling the entire fourth-year. Face florid and bathed in perspiration, his features were demented and his grey suit appeared as if he had spent a month in it sleeping rough.

The first time he catapulted from his seat, it was all going to blow. Those in the know – and there were quite a few by now judging by the number of heads turned towards Bill and his exploding tripod – were eagerly awaiting the demise of the chemist. The first hymn began with an unusual musical introduction which Bill liked; it was more suited to the Tower Ballroom than the solemnity of the mass.

Amazingly, Bill sat stock-still as if he feared that any movement would not just put him on his arse but blow him to smithereens. It became apparent that word was spreading as more and more of the congregation's eyes were fixed on Bill and the stool. The sung responses from the school, instead of being delivered in perfect tune, were starting to get a bit ragged and mumbled as the intensity of the situation began to affect the boys' concentration.

Halfway through the mass and still Bill was motionless. Then he made a couple of tiny jumps that were greeted with 'oohs' and 'aahs' that were clearly audible, causing Fr Duffy to turn and glare at us.

Bill seemed to be in a subdued mood as the mass came to its conclusion. But, when just about everyone had given up hope, Bill went into overdrive for the last hymn. He launched himself from his stool in a frenzied finale, so much so that a wave of 'whoahs' and 'here we gos' swept through the leering throng. When Bill landed again, the neatly sawn leg gave way with a great 'C-R-A-C-K' that reverberated throughout the old hall. The organ-playing Chemistry master was hurled backwards to great cheers. The stool flew in one direction, he went in the other. The kids were still laughing when the priest and altar boys rushed to Bill's aid.

When Bill landed in a heap, Sting and I had laughed along with the rest, though not as laboriously as some. When he didn't get back to his feet immediately, I experienced a sudden pang of guilt. Neither Sting nor I wanted Bill to be hurt. He was no spring chicken and he had come down with a tremendous thud. The school ghouls were now quiet, with only the most evil ones wanting to see Bill carted off to hospital.

In a moment of inspiration, Hemy managed to win over his enemies. As he lay on the ground, he shouted for all to hear, 'My leg... my leg is broken.' We looked at each other in shocked silence. Then Bill leaped to his feet in an instant, a good effort for a fat bloke, holding up the leg of the shattered stool, shouting, 'Here it is, my broken leg!' laughing as he brandished the chair-leg aloft to universal acclaim.

After a few minutes, calm was restored and we left the hall to continue the school day. We were all square now. We forgave Bill his clamp-wielding episode and any other grudges we held, either real or imagined.

Everyone was impressed by Bill's floorshow but when, in the next term, we were offered the choice between Chemistry and Geography, all but three pupils chose Geography. As a result, 'Wild' Bill Hemy never taught Sting or me again. Nor did Sting and I ever play 'Hang Man' again while Bill waffled on about hydrochloric acid taking the skin from the flesh and the flesh from the bone. Not that it mattered much since we were never allowed anywhere near that stuff anyway. Judging by some of the class's evil plans for Bill, it's as well for him that we were not.

15 – STING THE GOALIE

In the sixth-year, field trips up the Tyne Valley and to the Lake District developed into little more than an excuse to party. We always managed to slope off to the pub, leaving the Geography department to find us. Dragging us away from the bar sometimes proved next to impossible. On one famous trip to Cumbria, Sting and I, as well as a couple of our pals, managed to hide away almost all day in a little tavern before the Geography team tracked us down. They joined us for a drink. The reputation of this day out went before it and the school was awash with wild tales. Naturally, a further trip was organised for a study of the North-East coastline.

The organisers had, they thought, a cunning plan. They decided no longer to restrict the trip to senior boys; all were welcome, even first-years. I think the Geography masters considered that, if we had any sense of responsibility at all, we would not be diving off to the nearest pub when we had dozens of little schoolkids in tow. We would, of course, sadly let them down. Three busloads took off for the Northumbrian coast in the last week of term, July 1968. All examinations over with, we could enjoy our day trip in traditional style. Six masters were there to run the show – the whole of the Geography department.

We were supposed to walk along the beach from Whitley Bay to Tynemouth, while the Geography teachers lectured their pupils on the interesting facets of coastal erosion, sea-stacks, long-shore drift, etc. The seniors in the group were supposed to be looking after the youngsters. We did this with the minimum of inconvenience to ourselves, letting them scamper over rocks and explore the many caves they found.

'Hoy, sixer,' one of the young 'uns shouted at Sting. 'When are we going to the pub?'

'Soon, kidder,' Sting answered laconically, without breaking stride.

'Look over there at that sign. What does it say?' asked the little lad of Sting, pointing at a 'No Swimming' notice.

'Can't you read, man? It says, "Do not throw stones at this sign."' So thirty kids hurled pebbles at it. 'That's my boys,' Sting laughed.

Escape, however, was looking impossible. Masters and kids alike were watching the ringleaders like hawks. They were equally aware that we needed no excuse to take off and start a pub-crawl. We trudged along the beach for a while, staring at the cliff tops, looking for any possible way of quitting the scene but we were cornered. No one – not even the swots – appeared to be the slightest bit interested in what the bevy of masters was ranting on about. The day-trippers had degenerated into a straggling rabble. The Geography masters could be seen in the distance, pointing out things of geomorphic importance to one another. They argued with each other in their own little huddle as the kids dispersed along the shoreline.

But the senior boys had not exactly been diligent shepherds. By this time, the juniors had spread out to such a degree that some were only dots in the distance. Tony Hewson, showing a previously latent sense of duty, lolloped off, sheep-dog-style, to round the stragglers up. 'Away to me, come by, come by, away to me, lie down,' Sting shouted after him to loud laughs.

The mob finally made it to Tynemouth beach, where we were instructed to eat our packed lunches. Only a select few had brought anything to eat with them – such was the reputation of these field trips that everybody was confident they would be having a 'ploughman's lunch' in the pub, no matter how young they were.

We reckoned it was time to split. We were just about to make a bolt for the promenade when 'Noddy' Lunn spotted our group of conspirators, stopping us in our tracks. 'You gentlemen weren't thinking of leaving us, were you?' asked Lunn, knowing full well that was exactly what we were about to do.

'No, sir, not us, we just needed to use the toilet. All this sea air has had a detrimental effect on the bladder,' Bob Taylor explained weakly.

Poor excuses were his speciality. His reason for taking two days off earlier in the term had been couched in simple terms: 'I broke my thermos flask.' Bob reckoned that thermos flasks were the greatest invention ever. 'They keep hot things hot, and cold things cold. How do they always know which function to perform?'

Back on the beach, 'Plan B' was about to be put into action. If Mohammed couldn't come to the mountain… we would still have our liquid lunch.

We started a diversionary game of football on the sands, so that Tony and some third-year minions could slip off unnoticed up on to the promenade and buy as much lager from the nearest off-licence as our whip-round would run to. The diversion, however, was starting to become the main event of the day. The match on the beach had taken on titanic importance. A full 11-a-side game was in progress. The school First XI, who had just won the English Schools National Trophy, were pitted against a rag-bag team of former school-team players like myself and Trevor Dyson, plus assorted 'ne'er do wells'. Sting, who couldn't play the game to save his life, went in goal.

The match wasn't taken seriously by either side until the underdogs took the lead. Then it took on new meaning. With a hundred St Cuthbert's kids watching, all shouting for the 'stiffs', the cup-winners feared humiliation and started to play in earnest. As the game continued, holidaymakers sunning themselves on the beach also began watching, clapping good moves.

Considering the difference in ability between the two sides, the elite team should have been winning easily but, although they had scored twice to take a 2–1 lead at half-time, we still fancied our chances. Peter Barron, one of the masters, volunteered to referee the second half. At the start of the second half, to my total joy, I 'skinned' school captain, Hughie MacBride, and smashed home an unstoppable drive. I ran the length of the beach, waving to our ecstatic supporters before falling to my knees, making the sign of the cross.

Needle had now crept into the match as tackle after tackle, each one more illegal than the last, was ruled fair by the eccentric ref. The result of the game was now of paramount importance to both sides. We strove for a winner. Surprisingly, Sting, playing in goal, was an inspiration. His face set in concrete, he leaped to make great saves that were bemusing both sides alike. No one thought him capable of such a display. Someone argued later that they could only imagine that Sting was under the impression he was getting paid for his efforts.

All seemed lost when we were penalised by the clearly biased Barron, who awarded a penalty against us. Joe Bulman, felled by a 16-stone prop-forward leased from the rugby team, had flown through the air to such good purpose that shouts of 'Six', 'Six-and-a-half', 'Six', 'Seven', 'Six-and-a-half' and 'Six' came from diving judges on either side of the pitch.

A deathly hush descended upon the spectators. Joe stepped up and whacked the penalty kick hard and true towards the bottom corner, only to see Sting, 'The Puma', make a save Gordon Banks would have struggled to emulate, when he pushed Joe's shot wide of the pile of blazers which served as the goal-post.

Pandemonium followed, as he was mobbed by his team-mates, little lads who had invaded the pitch and even a couple of bathing beauties who had appeared from nowhere. The resultant corner (following Sting's save) was punched away by 'The Puma' straight to the feet of Trev Dyson who calmly rounded two England Boys trialists and stroked home the winning goal to scenes of mass hysteria. Now for some beer!

We fell upon the ice-cold lager, swilling it down with the minimum of fuss while the staff turned a blind eye. The supporters looked at us with envy as we slaked our thirst. Magnanimous in victory, we handed over a couple of bottles to be shared between a hundred or so of them. We were all heart! At the same time, we issued a strict injunction that no one under the age of seven should have a taste. After all, we were not morally bankrupt.

The beaten side, with as much lack of grace as we had expected, came to down a few beers. Joe's excuse for missing the penalty was that Sting had put him off because he looked like a 'poof'. As a joke, Sting had worn a leotard for the match, sticking to a promise he had made before the trip. This is obviously an excuse that Sir Alex Ferguson might want to incorporate in any future editions of his Book of Excuses, if there is room for another one.

We spent the rest of the afternoon sunbathing and drinking. Where the rest of the group had gone was a mystery. We tried looking in all the pubs along the sea front, manfully searching for a pub with a hundred underage drinkers inside it. It turned out that they had spent their time in various amusement arcades in Tynemouth – better than getting blind drunk, we thought, at least!

Back on the bus, the singing and dancing from those who were slightly intoxicated was a real eye-opener. Sting's version of the Rolling Stones' 'Honky-Tonk Women' went down like a lead balloon. I had absolutely no idea I knew how to dance the 'Mashed Potato' but, seemingly, I could all of a sudden. Mercifully, the bus was not going back to school. A lunatic tribe of overexcited, drunken sixth-formers marauding through the halls might not have gone down too well with the boss.

Those in charge of the trip had admitted defeat early on in proceedings, so little was said to criticise the boys. There were, however, no more Geography field trips. A baffling decision, we thought. How on earth were we supposed to learn about the countryside without such enterprises? It's no wonder Sting still thinks that 'Marsden Rock' is hard and red with the word 'Marsden' running through it, and I still can't tell a tarn from a tennis racket.

16 – GOD BLESS DERRY

As sixth-formers at the school, for some inexplicable reason we adopted the 'two-bit actor' Derren Nesbitt as our hero. He became an obsession with us. We formed a mini fan club and, when he appeared in a film or TV series, we discussed its merits at length, though never criticising our beloved Derry. The sixth-form room walls were lined with shelves of ancient books – biographies of obscure saints. They had been there since the Norman Invasion. So we decided to liven the place up a bit by rebinding the old volumes, giving the books new headings. *Mein Blond Kampf – The Life and Works of Derren Nesbitt*, one read. Another read, *Albino? No, Old Bean, Derren Nesbitt: A Critique*. So it went on, until virtually every book on the shelf was apparently devoted to the sainted Derren.

Our reverence came to a head when, on the last day of

term in the summer of 1968, Sting wrote on the blackboard in huge letters 'GOD BLESS DERRY' as a token of our appreciation of this giant among actors. A simple thought-provoking tribute from one Aryan to another, I thought. Just as Sting had finished his statement, in walked 'Poppa Cass' – the head. With the usual expression on his face like a Rottweiler with piles, he surveyed the graffiti on the board. He turned towards the class, asking who had defaced the blackboard with this proclamation.

He did have a point. After all, we were young men now. We really should have had more important things on our minds than Derry Nesbitt. The trouble was that, as almost all of us had brains the size of a pea, A-levels notwithstanding, we sadly did not have more important things on our minds.

To universal surprise, Sting owned up almost immediately. Even more surprisingly, the boss broached the subject with something approaching compassion. I was taken aback. Almost smiling, the head said, 'I sympathise with your sentiments, son, but devoting yourself to a cause not directly of your concern will never help the situation. Your love of Derry, though commendable, could be seen by others to be provocative. Now, please, wipe it from the board and keep your feelings, however deep, to yourself in future.'

We looked at each other stupefied, as Sting looked at the boss open-mouthed. What the hell was the old man on about? Sting's love for Derry was 'commendable', but might be seen as 'provocative'... The boss had lost the plot. He stared at Sting, presumably waiting for an answer to his comments about the clearly homosexual youth in front of him and his love for this young man called 'Derry', which the boss had so sensitively dealt with. Sting stood there, dumbstruck.

Then the penny dropped. Bob Taylor whispered just loud enough for Sting to hear, 'Christ Almighty, he doesn't think you mean Derry Nesbitt; he's on about Derry in Ireland... you know, Londonderry. He thinks you're making a political statement!'

Faced with having to conjure up a political conscience, Sting was still nonplussed. Before he got the chance to reply, an idiot stepped into the fray – an idiot of old, namely the crazed Spud Murphy, whose run-in with the boss years ago was still talked about.

'Excuse me, Father,' Murphy interrupted, a feeling of *deja vu* rippling through the class, 'it is not the City of Londonderry that Sumner is referring to but the actor, Derry Nesbitt.'

The boss knew the demented Murphy well and he was having none of it. 'Rubbish,' he shouted at the lad, 'you are doing it again, Murphy. Trying to make a fool of me. Are you saying that this reference is to an actor I have never heard of? Go to my room immediately, you buffoon,' he demanded.

'It's true, Father. Ask Sumner. Ask anyone if you don't believe me,' he argued.

'Get out!' the head ordered, but Murphy had an ace up his sleeve.

'Just look at one of the books on the shelf, Father. It will have a stupid title. Something to do with Derren Nesbitt' was his potentially lethal Parthian shot.

We all cringed at his outburst. Every book on that shelf was apparently devoted to Derren Nesbitt. I had written many of them myself. We held our breath waiting for the inevitable, as Spud stood in the doorway smirking. The boss picked up a book at random and read the title out loud. '*Saint Ignatius Loyola: The Society of Jesus.*' Murphy looked shell-shocked. We were just shocked. The boss, now convinced Murphy was at it again, commanded, 'Out! Now!'

Murphy gloomily ambled out, still crazy after all these years. He had had the audacity to tell the truth for possibly the first time in his life and it blew up in his face. It's just as well the boss did not go on to read the rest of the book's title as it read, 'By Derren "Face Like An Angel's Arse" Nesbitt'. Miracles do happen, we concluded.

Sting still had some explaining to do though. 'I'm afraid Murphy is out of his tree again, Father,' Sting said, a bit too cockily. 'You are, of course, quite right about my allegiances in the Province,' he said, lying through his teeth.

'You know, my son, my surname is Cassidy. I have deep feelings when it comes to the Emerald Isle. I suggest that you, like me, say nothing on the subject in future,' the head said to a nodding audience.

'Yes, of course, Father,' Sting concurred.

Despite Spud's treacherous attempt at sabotage, we had kept our secret. Many years later, when I saw the film *Quadrophenia*, in which Sting played the 'ace-face mod', I realised that he was playing Derren Nesbitt playing the ace face. He had carried his admiration of Derry into adulthood. I was well impressed.

I still smile when I watch the much-shown film *Where Eagles Dare*, when Derry – the eternal baddie, this time in the role of a Gestapo officer – gets blown away by Clint Eastwood (as does everyone else in the film for that matter). It always reminds me of those days in the sixth form – happy days.

17 – HAIRY REMOVES THE REMOVE

By the sixth-year, our clique of pals was bound together in tight-knit friendship. We had a common interest in anything that was frowned upon by the school authorities. Sting and I were told – separately and together – that we were the laziest buggers in the school. If that did not include the staff, this was fair comment. With a mixture of native cunning and sleight of brain, we attained almost identical O-level results. We both won places in Lower-Six Arts. A minimum of five O-level passes was required to secure a sixth-form place. About three-quarters of pupils who took the exams managed to achieve that goal. Those who did not either repeated their fifth year in the grandly named 'Five Remove' or left the school to join the real world.

To set the sixth form apart from the rest of the school, we wore black blazers, instead of the maroon ones we had worn for the previous five years, along with a black-and-maroon tie. The badge on our blazers was also slightly different. Those who repeated their fifth year were supposed to continue with the old maroon blazer, until that is Hairy Hetherington decided otherwise. After failing some of his O-levels, the lad with the incredible stammer, who must have taken a week out of my life while he talked to me, turned up for the new term wearing a black sixth-form blazer. Surely a hanging offence, if I was any judge.

What happened next was extraordinary. Instead of having his buttons snapped off, then his blazer dragged from his back by the boss '*pour encourager les autres*', not only was he allowed to continue to wear his illegal jacket but the rest of the remove were also told to wear black blazers. To put the tin hat on it, 'Five Remove' was retitled the much more prestigious 'Six Remove'.

It's not everyone who can say they created history at St Cuthbert's but Hairy did. For that, I will always remember him. The rest of us 'real' sixers went on very much as normal, shirking, slacking, wasting, wan... you get the picture. We studied only three subjects now. I took Geography, Maths and Economics, while Sting took Geography, English and Economics. I had originally intended to take Latin as one of my A-level subjects, mainly because I enjoyed it – unlike anyone else I knew – and because 'Genial Joe' Meadows, the Latin master, was the best-respected teacher at the school – a great bloke, who I even had the odd pint with in The Sun pub in Benton, Newcastle. When I told Sting what I was going to do, he answered by telling me that he fancied Early Etruscan, despite the fact that only three people in the world spoke it. I took his point and settled for Geography.

Over the years, my Maths masters had been universally good apart from the demonic Brannigan. Albert Cutter, Bill Mastaglio and Peter Kennedy had all helped me on my way to an O-level pass in the subject. For A-level Maths, Peter Kennedy had the doubtful privilege of teaching a dozen others and me part of our A-level course, the less demanding branch of Statistics; Pure Maths was left to a new teacher at the school, the lavishly named Mr ARW Dawe.

He was a diminutive guy, with boyish good looks, short, short hair and, almost unheard of for a St Cuthbert's master, an athletic build. He was, in fact, Northumberland County Tennis Champion, hence the physique. After our very first lesson with him, we concluded that he was the poshest man in Newcastle. He looked more like a financier than a teacher in his smart pin-striped suit with waistcoat and old-school tie (not St Cuthbert's) to match. Ashley, as some of the class called him to his face, was, as an old Geordie saying goes, 'as soft as shite'.

His 'it's your own time you're wasting' attitude was nowhere near stringent enough to drum the principles of Calculus into our thick skulls. Indeed, he could not have explained the concept with less clarity if he had conducted the lesson in Swahili. Ashley had no chance. My failure at the subject was a mere formality but I think I might have given my examiner a good laugh because some of the graphs I drew looked like massive erections.

Economics was a subject new to the school curriculum. A rather straight-laced master by the name of Peter Donaghy was teaching it to us. In his mid-30s and of average height and build, he had short dark hair and wore thick horn-rimmed specs. An able man who stood no nonsense, he guided Sting and me to similar pass marks at A-level. He gained new kudos when Newcastle United asked him to be their interpreter when they played Real Zaragoza in that season's European Fairs cup. As he spoke fluent Spanish, he offered his services and the club agreed. The result was a nice trip abroad and seats in the dugout for both home and away matches. He told the class the full story on his return and we lapped it up. Peter wasn't such a stuffed shirt, after all.

18 – OVER AND OUT?

Our time at St Cuthbert's was coming to a close but what remained of it did not pass without further shenanigans. The elite band of pals swore never to lose touch. This is usually easier said than done, so it is with some pride that I can say that the majority of us are close to this day. I see Hughie, Tony and Joe on a regular basis; Sting less so, but we still meet now and again and he phones me when he has no one on hand to argue with. Dave Bradshaw, Paul Elliot and John Shaw I see less often, but I still call them my friends. In September 1995, we celebrated our Silver Anniversary of leaving school by having a meal together in the plush San Lorenzo's restaurant in Knightsbridge, London.

Everyone turned up, including Sting. We even had a gatecrasher, my best pal Ronnie White, who knew all of us including Sting, and, although he never went to St

Cuthbert's, most people thought that he had. His excuse for intrusion was that he thought it was not an 'Old School' reunion but an 'Old Fools' reunion.

We did have some fun, though. Sting had hired a Memory Man, 'Malcolm Magic', to barge in on the party. Sting had armed him with info on each one of us, which he was using to pretend that he too had gone to St Cuthbert's and knew us all intimately. Sting greeted him warmly like he had known him all his life, while we looked on surprised as obviously we didn't know him from Adam. He talked to each of us in turn as he went round the table, saying things like, 'Hi, Hughie. How's your wife, Paddy?' When he got to Ron, he shouted, 'Who the fucking hell are you? I can't remember you from St Cuthbert's!' to howls of laughter, as we began to twig it was all a wind-up.

The last time we had all sat down to dinner, *sans* Ron and Malcolm, was at the school-leaving dinner 25 years previously. After the final examinations, it was a tradition at the school to lay on a dinner for those pupils who were on their way into the big, bad world outside.

For the first time in living memory, no instructions had been issued on what we were to wear. The result was some very interesting garb paraded by the class extroverts. This ranged from full evening dress to lederhosen. I was expecting Spud Murphy and his pal to come as a pantomime horse. In the event, Paul Elliot's gold lame suit was the most outrageous. He drew a few glares from the boss and the few other masters present but nothing was said. Sting, myself and the rest of the clique were models of sobriety in our best suits, collars and ties. Only Sting went slightly overboard by wearing spats, which he swore he had found on a bus.

After the meal, which was a darned sight tastier than anything I had previously sampled from the school kitchens, the boss gave us his farewell speech. I was distinctly nervous about this because unintentional humour was a big weakness of the boss. An adverse response from the leavers could turn the evening into one to forget. Was Spud, for instance, waiting for one last chance of revenge?

As many boys had discovered over the years, the Reverend Canon Martin Cassidy was not a man to ridicule lightly. He droned on for a while, bidding us a fond farewell by saying that we were as lazy a bunch as he had ever encountered, but adding the rider that because we had attained good pass rates in our exams then, all in all, we weren't such a bad lot. On the sports field we had been outstanding – particularly after the First XI had won the National Football Trophy – and he said he thought there might be a budding Jackie Milburn among us, an observation that showed his age.

Then he did what I had been dreading. He began to tell a 'funny story'. What is it about speech-makers that, no matter how serious the subject – be it disease, death or disaster – they feel obliged at some point to include a humorous anecdote? Does everyone, deep down, even someone as sombre as the head, want to be a comedian?

It certainly looked like it. The boss was determined to have his 'twopence worth'.

He was taking a risk with this audience, which included belligerent lads with grievances going back years and warmed arses to remind them of those. They might not react to his tale with polite laughter. I feared an embarrassing silence or even jeering. If he repeated his offer of a punch-up tonight as he had a few years back, the lads would race to form a queue. If no one laughed, I would and some sycophants might join me, I reckoned. Why I felt this to be my duty, I don't know. Perhaps I was destined for the Diplomatic Corps.

His funny story began. He said he knew that we had nicknames for many of the staff, not all of them complimentary. He waited for a laugh. There was silence. He continued by saying that he also knew that we all called him 'the boss', not the most startling of observations. If he had known that we also referred to him as 'Dracula', 'The Skull' and 'Doctor Death', he might not have been so amiable.

He carried on talking, saying that, when he was a young student, a French priest called Fr Dag Hibert taught him and that we would never be able to guess what the young scamps nicknamed him. If it had been anything other than 'Dicky Bird', I would show my arse in Fenwick's window, I mused. Before the Canon could give his obvious answer, saving me a conviction for indecent exposure, Sting turned to me and whispered, 'I bet they called him "Cunt Features".' I crumpled in a heap just as the boss said, 'Dicky Bird!' to no one's surprise, except, perhaps, Spud Murphy's.

I was the only member of the audience who even smiled, causing the head to look kindly in my direction as at least I seemed to have found his tale hilarious. Sting had me in the palm of his hand by now and he mercilessly followed up with: 'Do you know what we called the other French teacher, "Monsieur Pousse Cart"? We called him "Twat Features"! I bet you thought we called him "Pussy Cat", didn't you?'

By this time I was in convulsions, almost falling from my chair. The boss had not gone on to make any more 'witticisms' and my laughter echoed around the otherwise silent dining room. Irritated, the boss rounded on me. 'There is always someone who tries to spoil these occasions by acting the fool. Yes, you, Berryman, isn't it?' he shouted at me, the one person who didn't want to spoil the occasion. 'I think that I and the rest of the diners would like you to leave if you can't behave yourself,' he told me, as a lad wearing dungarees and a cowboy hat stood up, calling for my arrest – to my great annoyance.

I stood up and faced him, pleading, 'I'm so sorry, Father. I didn't mean to offend you.'

He glared at me for what seemed like ten minutes before continuing with his speech. Despite Sting still trying to wind me up, I managed to control myself until the boss had finished to a lukewarm round of applause, which sounded suspiciously like a slow handclap. When we left the dining room, he shook everyone's hand including mine and even Spud's but he didn't look me in the eye.

Yet again, the boy Sting had messed me around and blighted the last thing I ever did at the school. He nearly had me expelled on the last day of my education! Sting treated me to Smokey Robinson's 'Tears of a Clown' as we trudged away from the school for the very last time. I forgave him his trespasses, as I had done on all the other occasions. Forgiven, but not forgotten...

19 – KNEES, KNEES, KNEES!

Stan Eardley and Tony Knox were the two Games masters at the school while Sting and I were there. Stan had been at the school since God knows when, whereas Knoxy arrived during our time there. Stan wore a cream (though it might have started out white) cricket sweater all year round. He looked the very image of a captured World War II fighter pilot, right down to his wavy Brylcreemed hair. Knox – although the same height as Stan which was about five feet eight – had a muscled appearance, wiry and tough. Balding with a prominent Roman nose, he cut an imposing figure.

Stan had a phenomenal memory. He could name every boy in the school correctly. Tony was not quite as good and called me 'Burryman' all the time. Tony was a football coach and played football at a high level, winning several amateur caps for England. Stan was a winger in the Stanley Matthews mode but he struggled to get into the school-staff team. He really did have his own ideas about the game.

It's fair to say that Stan wasn't trying to coach a side to win the World Cup and 90 per cent of the raw talent that he saw would never make any representative side, but some of his ideas were verging on the insane. Teaching first-year boys to play football is a harder task than it sounds. Those who are any good soon get bored with the simple passing and trapping routines others need, while those who are useless at the game will never be any good and would rather be in the class reading a comic or eating a jam sarnie.

Trapping the ball with the sole of the foot was too simple for Stan. He actually invented his own way of trapping the ball. He called it 'trapping with the knees'. In 37 years of playing and watching the beautiful game, I have never seen anyone try to repeat Stan's folly outside of his Games lesson. According to Stan, you could trap the ball by pinning it to the ground with the knee. When he demonstrated this fascinating piece of skill, he actually trapped the ball with his shins, not his knees – when you think about it, if you trapped with the knees, you would be virtually kneeling on the ball. Nevertheless, 'trapping with the knees' he called it. It was an impossible manoeuvre, more suited to a circus than the soccer pitch. Stan would oversee games played by fat kids and specs-wearers and would scream, 'With your knees!' as the ball flew towards them. They had more chance of winning the Grand National than complying with Stan's wishes.

The most spectacular own goal I ever saw came about when a defender tried to put Stan's extravagant advice into practice. As the ball reached the lad, down went his knees in a brave but ultimately disastrous attempt at 'trapping with the knees'. The ball bounced off the top of his kneecap and shot into the back of his own net. 'Good try, lad,' shouted Stan. 'Very unlucky!' as his team-mates went across to him to slap him round his head.

I was a fast, bustling centre-forward, ultimately lacking the ball control to make any Football League scouts sit up and take notice. I did, though, score a hatful of goals in my school soccer career. Only when I was in the sixth form was I dropped from the side that went on to win the national championship. Merely a coincidence, of course!

20 – SLAPPED DAFT

Knees were definitely Stan's favourite part of the body. Not only had he brought the ridiculous 'knee-trapping' to the school but the even more daunting 'knee-boxing', too. Even before I attended the school, I had been told that I would be required to take part in bouts of 'knee-boxing'. I imagined that boxing gloves were strapped to your knees and you'd be faced by a similarly equipped boy four stones or so heavier than you and six inches taller. Then I thought you would be instructed to try and knee each other in the bollocks, until one of you was rendered unconscious. That, I presumed, would be me.

What this pastime actually involved was less pugilistic but in its own way just as violent. In a one-on-one confrontation, boys would square up to each other in the gym and attempt to smack their opponent on the knees with the palm of the hand. Just as 'trapping with the knees' had little to do with the knees, so it was with 'knee-boxing' – the thighs were actually the targets for the 'knee-boxers'. Stan really should have consulted a therapist about his 'knees' fixation.

Warming up in the gym before Games lessons, the class would suddenly hear Stan's blood-curdling yell of 'Knee boxing', and the boy nearest to you would take up the cudgels, face you, then try and slap your legs as you did likewise. What this was supposed to achieve, other than sore legs, was a mystery to me. Invariably, when I saw who my opponent was, my heart sank. It was always some kid, with hands like matured hams, who despised me – someone who was totally useless at any recognised sport but who could have represented England Under-21s at 'knee-boxing'. Often the bouts would leave me with what appeared to be second-degree burns on my legs. Why Stan didn't just give us all a knife each and encourage us to slash at each other's scrotums, I don't know. He would probably have called it 'knee-gashing' given his obsession with that part of the body.

After several of these thrashings – some of which occurred on days when I was supposed to be playing for the school football team – I grew more and more desperate to avoid them. After all, I argued, you didn't see players in a warm-up before a match trying to maim their team-mates – well, not very often. I didn't see why I should be leading the attack with my legs the colour of Neapolitan ice cream.

I noticed that Sting had been similarly injured as a result of these 'knee-boxing' exhibitions. We had never hooked up for this activity before as we didn't want to have to whack each other. We were friends, after all. I told him of my hatred for the sport, suggesting to him that the only conclusion was to contrive to partner each other with mutual vows of pacifism. We could pretend we were hard at it without ever landing a blow in anger.

He agreed to put the plan into practice as soon as possible. The gym, which at the time doubled as a dining room, smelled permanently of boiled cabbage and made me feel quite ill. Sting and I stuck together like two 'straights' at a gay pyjama party. Duly came the shout from Stan: 'Knee boxing!' Sting and I faced one another immediately before the fat lads could move in. The plot worked a treat. We launched ourselves at each other, snarling and grimacing, in a possibly over-the-top show of aggression. It must have looked contrived to anyone watching closely as each one of our blows came to an abrupt halt inches away from its target.

With nearly twenty couples to supervise, Stan could only see our lurches and hear the slaps landing on the thighs of the daft sods that were playing this mad game for real. The bouts only lasted a few minutes, which was just as well as otherwise kids could have ended up in callipers. But we had succeeded in our charade and vowed to use it every time in future. The ruse worked so well that none of the other 'knee-boxers', some with hands like table-tennis bats, dared claim Sting or me as their partner. Stan never noticed what was happening, so all was well as we continued using the scam to our hearts' content. One day the pot cracked.

We had just gone into a matinee performance, when I noticed Stan looking at us from a distance. I feared that he had rumbled our wheeze but, before I could warn my partner, Stan was right beside us, standing just behind Sting. I tried signalling with my eyes – rolling them about like a loon – that something was afoot, but Sting wasn't looking at my face. He was just about to jump at me in a mock attempt at a thigh-stinging blow that was going to look all too phoney to the hovering Stan. So I swayed away from his no-blow, then gave him a real stinger on the fleshy part of the inside of his thigh. Cruel to be kind, I thought. Sting was livid. 'You twat,' he spat out through clenched teeth as Stan wheeled away satisfied there was a real bout in progress.

'No, man! I didn't want to hit you. Stan was watching!' I insisted, but Sting looked up to see Stan, now yards away, looking in the opposite direction.

Sting returned my blow with interest, catching me in the same spot I had got him. Game on! Our friendship lost in that moment, we stalked each other round the gym, faces set, teeth bared. We proceeded to give the finest and most violent exhibition of 'knee-boxing' ever witnessed. Lost in that crazy world that Stan had invented, the game's two sternest critics were giving it all they had. All reason gone, we scampered round the arena thwacking each other's legs into submission.

The rest of the boxers had packed up minutes earlier. As the titanic battle continued, they now stood in awe as we exchanged blows oblivious to anything other than the fight. Eventually our legs looked like they had been attacked with a wire brush and Stan finally intervened. 'That's enough, boys. Very well done.'

We stopped the savagery as Stan went off to organise more mayhem, then collapsed to the ground in agony.

'I hope you're bloody well pleased with yourself,' I chided as Sting looked me in the face for the first time since the main event.

'Me?' he replied. 'You're the one who started it in the first place.'

I was too exhausted to argue. We hauled each other to our feet and both burst out laughing. 'No hard feelings?' I said to Sting.

'No feelings at all. I'm numb from the waist down,' he replied.

We shook hands and he accepted my explanation this time. Surely Stan would never question the authenticity of our fights in future. Nearly crippling one another was surely proof enough – what more could Stan ask for?

During the next gym lesson, we joined up for some non-combative combat. Stan leaped between us. 'No, not this time, you two. You take it far too seriously.'

We looked at each other in stupefaction and groaned to see some leering half-wits with hands like fucking tennis rackets eyeing us up with evil intent.

21 – IT'S A GAME OF ONE HALF, BRIAN

Growing up in Longbenton, I always assumed that everyone could play football, much as I assumed that everyone could read and write. It wasn't until I attended St Cuthbert's that I realised there were boys who were incapable of playing the game and, far worse, some who did not like the game and would not play it at all.

In our third year, I was the house football captain and, despite the fact that there were fifty or so pupils in our house, Cunningham's, finding a side of 11 decent players was a tricky proposition. Only four of us were up to scratch: the goalie, Michael Robinson, a well-spoken lad; Steve Harvey, who went on to become 'head boy'; Denny Allen, a crazy young lad, and me, the ever-modest Jim Berryman. The rest of the side was only there to make up the numbers, willing workhorses who ran their socks off for the team. I remember one day in particular which turned out to be a black day for the sport.

The team was missing three regulars due to the flu and I could barely pick a side for the house match against School House. Yes, I know it's confusing calling one of the houses 'School'. Sting would often tell people he played football for the 'School' team. He did not; he merely played for School House and only once at that. It's like owning a racehorse and calling it 'Racehorse'. Lack of imagination was rife. Only after the boss died, when we were no longer pupils, was School House renamed Cassidy House.

I managed to convince two flu victims to play, as the game meant more to me than their health and I told them they should think the same way. I argued that, if they were really ill, they would not have been at school anyway. Ten up, one to go! I decided to put an invitation up on the school notice board, asking any Cunningham's House members who fancied a game to contact me.

I took the precaution of adding the proviso: 'No fat kids'. I wanted someone who could run, not stand in the centre-circle scoffing a bag of doughnuts while considering the art of 'trapping with the knees'.

Sadly, only one volunteer came forward, a lad I had seen around the school, standing alone, talking to himself. I can't recall his name, but I remember just everything else about him. He came from a middle-class family and he was skinny with very short, yet still tousled hair. He wore National Health Service glasses, which barely hid a magnificent squint.

I recalled seeing him marching to school, alone of course, bent well forward under the massive weight of his rucksack. Wearing the inevitable short trousers, he would have been more at home wandering about the Hindu Kush. All in all, he could not have been worse material if he had been up to his waist in a plaster cast. He wasn't fat though, so he was going to have to do. When I told him he was in, he grinned hideously then sprinted off, presumably to send a telegram to his proud parents.

Come match day, I was resigned to a crushing defeat until I found out that our opponents, School House, were having similar problems in fielding a decent side. In the changing room, I spotted a familiar figure donning a School House football top. It was the boy Sting. He may not have been fat or bespectacled and indeed could run like buggery, but his ball control was non-existent and his passing and crossing were even worse. I greeted him with open arms. I told him how pleased I was to see that his excellent prospects had been noted and his skills had won him a place among his peers.

He answered with a cheery, 'Go fuck yourself!'

I laughed, but the laughing stopped when Sting pointed to my new signing and said, 'If you think I'm useless, what the frigging hell is that?' I looked over at the debutant. He was sitting alone, munching a doorstep sarnie full of tomato ketchup which was slopping on to the changing-room floor.

'Hello, skipper,' the newcomer greeted me, more sauce hitting the deck as he stood up. I forgot how messy his lunch looked as I began to take in the rest of my full-back's appearance. His purple house football-shirt was buttoned to the neck as if he was just about to add a cravat. His shiny white shorts stretched well below his knees yet rose to his chest. Looking down, it didn't get any better. Instead of Cunningham's House socks, he wore a very old and tattered pair of green, hooped things, which were filled not just with his weedy legs but with what seemed like a volume of the *Encyclopaedia Britannica* in each sock. 'I haven't got any shin-pads, boss. Dad said to stuff paper down them,' he told me, as he saw me glowering at his elephantine calves. To complete the sorry picture, he wore an antique pair of football boots, the likes of which I had only seen before in a museum. Given the boots and the contents of the socks, he must have nearly doubled his body weight in the changing room. We were going to have to carry him on to the pitch!

The only new item of attire he wore merely served to emphasise this vision of clown-like excess. Long pristine laces were threaded through his antediluvian boots, surely last worn in a house match by his great-great-grandfather in 1907. It seemed he could never have worn football boots before because, instead of correctly tying the laces around the boots several times to take up the slack, he had simply tied them into enormous bows that drooped to the floor six inches on either side of his feet. Fine, if he was planning on sitting there all day, but, if he wanted to move, he would have fallen flat on his face. I was in despair. There was only one thing for it. I tied his boots properly for him, removed the reading material from his socks and unbuttoned his shirt. Now he only looked a shambles rather than a catastrophe.

'I can't play without my specs, skipper,' he said, as if I might have other ideas.

'Look,' I said in my most patronising voice, 'I'm playing you at left-back. When the ball comes to you, just kick it back up the field – whatever way our team is facing, not the way that you might be facing. Don't try to pass the ball or dribble. When our opponents have got possession – that's them in the white shirts – try and get it from them. You mustn't pick the ball up and you mustn't push them or kick them. Try and win the ball fairly in the tackle. OK?'

The new boy looked at me and nodded. To my consternation, so did the rest of my team, who thought this advice was directed at them as well. 'Right on, boss,' they shouted back at me. My heart was in my full-back's boots.

The game started and, within a couple of minutes, we were two goals behind – the first a powerful shot from Jimmy Hennegan and the second, unbelievably, from Sting. My full-back had stood rooted to the spot as Sting had strolled by him to toe-poke a weak drive past our keeper. Sting ran to the touchline, punching the sky in triumph. I felt physically sick.

The game was being played at the bottom of the school playing fields with another pitch to our left stretching to the edge of the school grounds. When a loose ball was punted towards my trusty defender, he did as instructed and managed to kick the ball back where it had come from. I latched on to the pass, slipped the ball to Steve Harvey and he rattled it into the back of the net.

We now had the bit between the teeth and were pressing for an equaliser. Sting, though, was off again. This time the bespectacled full-back from Hell hit him with a tackle that nearly sliced him in two. Sting went down like a bag of cement. 'No foul,' ruled the referee, the full-back's cousin.

'Well played, bonny lad,' I shouted to the new hero, looking down at the mangled Sting and smiling. The demented defender then set off after the ball, presumably to retrieve it so the opposition could take their throw-in, a show of sportsmanship rare in these house matches. I was wrong.

Taking no notice of the touch-line or the fact that the ball was out of play, the lunatic caught up with the ball yards away from the pitch and punted it with his pensioned-off boots even further into the distance. He was now over a hundred yards from the field of play. He ran after his kick, met the ball again and whacked it once more. Eventually he and the ball were almost out of sight; he was playing his own game on his own field. The gawky kid finally stopped when he was only a couple of yards short of the perimeter fence. Then he picked the ball up and began the long walk back up the field. He reached us five minutes later, by which time both teams were seated on the ground, waiting patiently for the loony's return. It should have been half-time but the bell rang out to signal a premature end to proceedings. The match was rearranged for the following week – we lost 4–0.

The result of the original game was posted on the notice board as follows: 'MATCH ABANDONED: NUTTER STOLE THE BALL'. How true.

22 – THEY THINK IT'S ALL OVER, HE IS *NOW*

St Cuthbert's had a strong tradition of excellence in sport, which was not that surprising, considering the cream of Catholic talent that the school had at its disposal. I represented the school at football and athletics, while Sting had a place in the rugby team, although, as far as I can recall, they never actually won a game. He was, though, a sprinter of some ability. He represented the City and the County and came within a whisker of a place in the national Under-17 side.

Within the school itself, sporting events between the different houses were keenly contested. During our time, there were six houses: my house was Cunningham's, Sting's was School House and we competed along with Mann's, Magill's, Wickwar's and Jeffrey's. They were all named after former headmasters – that was why School House was eventually renamed Cassidy House. Apart from that one ridiculous game of football, Sting and I had never faced each other in any sports competition. He specialised in the 100 yards and I did the 440 yards, so we never met head to head. We were sometimes pitted against one another in the 4x100 relay but as I always led off and he took the anchor, or last leg, we were never in direct competition. We did eventually meet in competition but it was not at school.

At youth level, local harriers clubs were popular but neither Sting nor I were members other than during a brief flirtation when we first realised we could run a bit. The strict training regimes seemed too much like hard work for a bone-idle pair like us. The large factories on Tyneside also organised athletics meetings, mainly for their annual sports day, when relatives of the employees were also invited to take part. Though strictly forbidden by the Amateur Athletics Association, small amounts of prize money were on offer along with various prizes and gift-vouchers. This was much more up my street.

In the summer of 1966, I entered the Formica Annual Sportsday 100-yards event. As my dad worked there, I was perfectly entitled to take my place in the line-up. I had received a programme of events the day before, perusing it mainly to see if I knew the name of anyone else who had entered for 'the 100-yards dash'. I had a good memory for the names of anyone who had turned me over in inter-school matches, and I just wanted to make sure I wasn't taking on someone who had run all over me previously. But I was no 100-yards champion and only took on the event because that was the only sprint distance on the agenda.

Talking of the 100-yards dash, why was the word 'dash' used to describe the event? Was there another way of running the event without having to dash? Besides, long-distance events weren't usually described as the 'three-mile saunter' or the 'six-mile loiter'. 'Dash' I would, then. It looked like I would have to dash three times to take the title of Formica Under-15 100-yards Champion. The event was scheduled in three stages: heats, semi-finals and final.

I was disgusted to note in the programme that there were also some events that had no place at a proper meet, such as egg-and-spoon races and the sack race. Not only that, but prizes of equal value were on offer for these non-events. I scanned the programme to see if my dad and I were entered for the Father and Son's Wheelbarrow race. I would have drawn the line at that.

The day of the meeting was also an important one for another sporting reason. It was the opening game of the 1966 World Cup – England v Uruguay at Wembley. The game – like all the others in that competition which was being held in England for the first and only time – was being televised live on the BBC. This was the reason for the poor turn-out of competitors that greeted me when I arrived at the start for my heat. I was the only competitor to show up.

For some inexplicable reason, I was still expected to run. I needed to finish in the first two in order to qualify for the semi. It was a damned close-run thing but I pulled through. I was in the semis and well pleased with my battling performance so far. I was told the semi would be a lot harder for me, as this time I was expected to run against other athletes. In the semi-final itself, farce was again the winner. Only four semi-finalists were there for the race and four qualified for the final. Yet again, I was expected to run despite the fact I could have hopped the distance and still qualified. Was it too late for the egg-and-spoon race?

I glanced along the starting line-up of opponents, only to see that none of them was kitted out for a sprint. I stood there in my St Cuthbert's running vest, immaculate white shorts and adidas running spikes. The rest were in various outfits, none of which was appropriate for any sort of sporting event.

I had seen better-dressed rag-and-bone men. One wore a floral shirt, industrial jeans and sandals, while another turned out in a wide-lapelled, three-piece suit, finished with brown brogues. He even kept his jacket on. The lad next to me was under four feet tall, looked about ten years old and wore the most ragged red woollen jumper I had ever seen. He was in short trousers – though these were not exactly short – with size-12 hobnailed boots complete with steel toecaps. I thought that I had strayed on to the set of *The Goon Show*. As I stood and looked at this motley crew lined up alongside, incredibly it was me who came in for criticism.

The starter turned to me and said quite seriously,

'You don't seem to be entering into the spirit of things, do you, son? What chance have these poor souls got with you in that gear? It's not the bloody Olympics, you know!'

I couldn't believe my ears. I was being bollocked for taking it too seriously. 'I can't remember being told the race was to be run in fancy dress,' I replied with as much sarcasm as I could muster. I could hear the others agreeing with him but I ignored them.

'On your marks,' said the starter as I took the orthodox stance for the sprint, fingertips on the line, hunched into a ball, ready to explode away from this charade.

'Get-set-go,' he shouted in one, catching me completely unawares. I was expecting a starting pistol. It didn't fool the others, though, as they ran off ever so slowly. I was left looking vainly at the starter who merely said, 'Go on then, get going!' The other lot were at least twenty yards ahead before I set off after them but I caught the sluggish band before halfway and at the tape I was some thirty yards in front. The guy with the suit stopped to light a fag but ran on to take third.

'Well done, son,' said my dad, 'but I think you had better sharpen up your start. They left you for dead early on, you know.'

I didn't reply. Surely in the final I would meet someone who could give me some sort of test. I watched the other semi-final. It was no better. A lad wearing wellies and a leather jacket romped away with it. Some daft kid even competed in a sack, mistaking it for his own event – he finished third.

Before the final, the starter approached me and asked if I would take off my running spikes and compete in bare feet to give the others a chance. I replied by cockily informing him that, to give this lot a chance, I would have to run in concrete slippers. I declined his offer, while the thought passed through my mind that, if this had been a cricket match and I was the only one wearing pads, I should have been asked to face the bowling with a chair-leg instead of a bat! The starter just sniffed and moved away. I was allowed to continue – very decent of him, I don't think!

The final was the formality I had anticipated. The lad, who erroneously got to the final hopping in a sack, was given his chance and finished second. 'I would have pissed that fucking sack-race,' the kid said to me on pulling up. No doubt about that. I won a leather wallet and a gift voucher for £5. I was still a bit put off by the fact that a majority of the watching crowd seemed to think I was some kind of snob, ruining a fun day out by turning the race into a procession, but my dad told me that any competition should be taken seriously and to take no notice. So that's exactly what I did.

The England v Uruguay match was goalless, so we hadn't missed much. My next opportunity to secure another title was at another factory's sports day, scheduled for the same day as the World Cup Final. This far ahead, I wasn't too concerned about the clash of dates as, judging from what had gone before, England had no chance of reaching the final. Wrong!

England duly reached the final where they would play West Germany. Now I was faced with the stark choice of either watching the match on TV or running at the meeting. I couldn't do both.

For a couple of days, I agonised before deciding to further my career as a semi-professional sprinter. I hadn't seen a full list of the runners for my event beforehand or I would have noticed a familiar name in the line-up: GM Sumner, City and County 100-yards Champion as well as my best pal and team-mate in the St Cuthbert's 4x100 school relay team. The sad truth is I could not beat him if I wore roller skates and he ran in Cuban heels.

The World Cup Final's appeal drastically limited the turn-out of competitors: there would be no heats, only a final. This was to be held between seven lads who had given up the chance to watch the most important football match in the nation's history.

'What the bloody hell are you doing here?' Sting asked me when I saw him, and he saw me, at the starting line.

'Me... what about you? I can't recall you saying you would be poncing about with some low-lifes this Saturday.'

'Well, I am, by the looks of things. What about you?'

'My dad runs the jellied-eels stall,' I lied.

Whatever the reason, he was there and it looked like I was about to lose my 100 per cent record. We agreed to run even though neither of us liked the idea much – me because I didn't want to lose, and he because he thought I would storm off in a huff when he won.

We were called to our marks. Sting, dressed like me in full running kit, looked along the line to see his rivals as eccentrically attired as mine had been in my first run with the parallel-world athletes. Sting was drawn in the next lane to me and he just shrugged his shoulders in mute agreement that we would race against each other and the rest of the cast of *Monty Python's Flying Circus*.

Soon we were off and running. I got a good start and was in front, with Sting only a little way behind. Someone else was almost on terms as well, a tall lad with a huge mop of bouncing ginger hair. He was wearing a massive pair of purple flares which billowed in the breeze. This was ridiculous. How could anyone run so fast while wearing loons and sandshoes?

At the halfway stage, Sting was in front of me and, to my horror and amazement, so was the guy with the flares. Still twenty yards from the tape, my eyes were fixed on the flapping turn-ups ahead of me. Then, for the only time in my athletics life, I fell flat on my face in a desperate attempt to overhaul the kid in the shimmering strides. Few though the spectators were, I could still hear peals of laughter at my unintentional acrobatics. Then I suddenly felt a hand helping me to my feet. I thought it was my dad but it was Sting. He had stopped when he saw me out of the corner of his eye crashing to the deck. He later told me that he had only stopped as the ginger git in the flares was going to 'do' him. My dad told me it was rubbish: Sting was clear and would have won. This kind of act was typical of Sting as a young boy and, in later years, as a man.

'Come on, let's get changed and piss off. We might catch the second half of the World Cup Final,' Sting urged as Ginger went on a lap of honour.

So we had had our head-on battle with its unusual outcome. Back at Wembley, England were doing the business, sending a singing nation into ecstasy.

23 – PULL YOUR FINGER OUT, MCBRIDE

Sting was Northumberland County 100-yards champion for two consecutive years, 1965 and 1966. I can vividly remember his first victory. At the starting line, he looked decidedly out of place, as if he had strayed on to the track from behind the counter of a hot-dog van.

Unlike his rivals who sported shiny new tracksuits, he wore an old, threadbare grey sweater over his running vest and a pair of Harold Abrahams-style, hand-me-down running spikes. He attracted wry looks from his smartly dressed opponents, who had an excellent view of him during the race as well – of his backside, to be more precise. He raced away from them to an emphatic victory, cheered to the rafters by the St Cuthbert's lads. My own performance in the 440 yards brought the team back down to earth with a bump as I could manage no better than fifth in the County 440-yards final.

As I was a good bend runner, I was chosen to lead off the 4x100 relay squad for the school. The team comprised Sting, myself, Hughie McBride and a lad a year younger than us called Bill Curly. We had enjoyed some success in the relay over the previous couple of years but we had never been able to beat the Royal Grammar School, Newcastle. We had competed against them on a number of occasions but victory had always eluded us. We were perennial runners-up. Now the City School Championships had come round again. The junior, intermediate and senior competitions all took place on the same day in mid-summer. Although a St Cuthbert's team always won at least one of the championships, and sometimes two, we had never won all three at the same time.

Now we were seniors – and had been in the same relay team together for two years – we could have passed the baton on to each other blindfolded. Sting, myself, Hughie and Bill operated like a well-oiled machine, yet we were still unable to vanquish the Royal Grammar lot. In 1967, the championships were held at Rutherford School, just up the road from St Cuthbert's. We had done exceptionally well. Our team coach, Games master Tony Knox, was beside himself with glee when we wrapped up the junior and intermediate competitions.

The seniors had done well, too. Sting won the 100 yards. Hughie had only lost in a desperate finish to the

220 yards, and I ran second in the 440 yards as well. The title was in the balance up to the last minute. When Kev Kavanagh won the mile for St Cuthbert's, it became apparent that, if we won the relay, we would take an unprecedented grand slam of titles.

However, the dreaded Royal Grammar stood in our way yet again. Tony Knox gathered the relay team together for one final pep talk. In hushed tones, he told us what it meant to him. We had to win it not just for him, the team and ourselves but also for the school, Catholics everywhere, St Cuthbert, the seraphim, cherubim, angels, archangels and the Pope. Or, at least I think he said that. I wasn't actually listening. I was watching Hughie fiddling about with the baton, a six-inch-long, hollow metal tube that I would soon hold in my hands while I ran like the wind and the entire Catholic world held its breath.

We were called to our marks and it felt like hundreds of spectators were watching, though only the St Cuthbert's contingent wanted us to win. As I was to lead off, I went over to Hughie and asked him for the baton. He gave me a sheepish grin, before saying – quite calmly, given the circumstances – that the baton was stuck on his finger. I told him that this was no time to be arsing around. With a feeling of impending doom, I quickly realised he was in earnest. He held out his hand to reveal the baton stuck fast on his right index finger. I yanked at it sharply to no avail.

Think! What to do? We might be forced to withdraw.

What would the Pope say? I knew what the boss would do: he would order a ceremonial burning at the stake. Should we ask for another baton? Or should we just tear the bastard's finger off? We settled on a solution that was just a touch insane. We would swap our running order, so that Hughie could lead off, then I would pull the baton from his finger as we were moving at pace. Simple.

Sting ambled over to see what was going on. He surveyed the scene, almost nonchalantly examining the welding of Hughie's finger to the unyielding piece of metal. He took charge. 'I'll get this fucker off,' insisted Sting. 'I'll take the second leg, Jim. You take mine, and Bill can do the last. OK?'

We hastily rearranged our running order. The finest moment in the history of school athletics was about to end in total chaos. I went to my new mark on the third leg. In the distance, I could hear Knoxy shouting. 'Where are you all going? Keep to your designated positions!' We ignored him. I fancied the odds of me ever seeing the baton at over a million to one.

The starter fired his pistol and Hughie was away, bonded to the unrelenting piece of aluminium. I was convinced that Hughie was in mortal danger of losing his finger when Sting grabbed the baton from him, so much so that my legs were like jelly. Hughie made a flying start and took an early lead. He slowed a little as he approached Sting who had a 'maniacal look on his face', Hughie said later. Sting, running, tugged violently at the baton. It never budged. He pulled Hughie along for ten yards or so, near to the disqualification zone, when by the grace of God finger and baton separated – mercifully Hughie was free and his finger was still attached to his hand.

Sting had lost a bit of ground during the wrestling stage and he was only third when he passed the baton on to me. 'Mind Hughie's finger,' Sting shouted at me as I grabbed the baton. I even looked closely at it just to make sure he was joking. The relief of receiving the baton intact spurred me on and I went like stink, adrenaline surging through my body. I ran like I have never run before, with the possible exception of when I was being chased by a gang of skinheads in Coventry.

When I passed the baton on to Bill Curly, a big, ginger, immensely powerful young lad, he was in second place and that's where we were destined to finish, or so I thought. To everyone's amazement, young Curly caught the Royal Grammar lad, the national Schools 220-yard Champion, then 'done him' right on the wire. He was chaired from the track to scenes of pure joy from all of the St Cuthbert's team and supporters. Tony Knox was overjoyed. His teams had done the unthinkable. We had won *the lot*! I haven't forgotten that day, and neither has Sting, Hughie or Bill either, I bet.

We reached the zenith of our athletics careers that afternoon, slipping relentlessly downhill ever after. Sting is still as fit as a lop and can still run a bit. I'd be lucky to go fifty yards without collapsing, but on that summer's day I did my bit and Hughie can still knock nails in with his horribly calloused index finger.

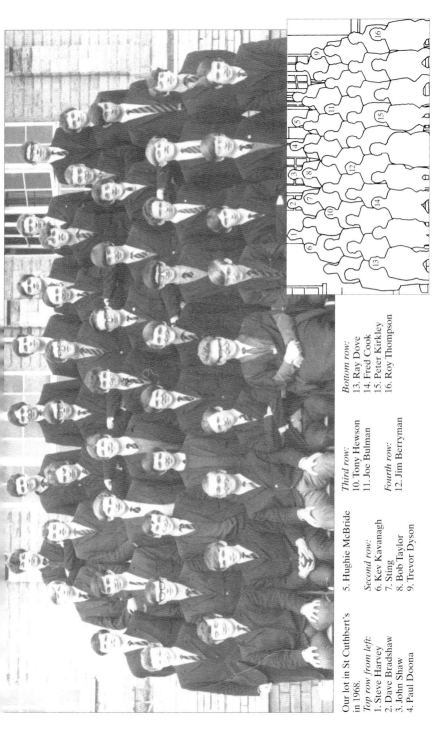

Our lot in St Cuthbert's in 1968.

Top row from left:
1. Steve Harvey
2. Dave Bradshaw
3. John Shaw
4. Paul Doona
5. Hughie McBride

Second row:
6. Kev Kavanagh
7. Sting
8. Bob Taylor
9. Trevor Dyson

Third row:
10. Tony Hewson
11. Joe Bulman

Fourth row:
12. Jim Berryman

Bottom row:
13. Ray Dove
14. Fred Cook
15. Peter Kirkley
16. Roy Thompson

At Sting's wedding, Trudie in the middle with, on her left, Kate Bradshaw (Dave's wife) and Paul Elliot on the right. Behind them are Ike and Tina Turner (only kidding!).

Top: Me with Sting and, *bottom*, with Paddy McBride (Hughie's wife) and Trudie at the wedding with Sting.

Sting's wedding: I'm in the middle with Hughie McBride on the left and my 'girlfriend' for the night, Ron White, on the right.

Top row, Paul Elliot, Sting, me and Dave Bradshaw in San Lorenzo's restaurant, London. It's 1995, 25 years since we left St Cuthbert's and the ex-inmates are still smiling (even the one in the electric chair, John Shaw)!

Above: Sting with Joe Bulman and Hughie McBride at San Lorenzo's.

Below: On the front lawn at Lake House, Sting plays with his daughter Coco.

Mr Jim Berryman

STING

requests the pleasure of your company

at a lunch to celebrate his award of the C.B.E.

on Thursday 9th October 2003

at Harry's Bar

26 South Audley Street, London W1

Drinks: 12.45pm
Lunch: 1.30pm
Dress: Smart, Casual or Scruffy

R.S.V.P.
...626090

Save the Date!
Jim
Sting's 50th Birthday Party

28th–30th September 2001

Marrakech
Morocco

If you know that you are unable to join us
please telephone

Invitations, accommodation details
and further information will follow

Sting requesting the pleasure of my company – though the Moroccan trip never went ahead due to the attacks on the World Trade Center.

The river Avon runs through the grounds of Lake House, Sting's home in Wiltshire.

24 – WHO WAS KING BILLY ANYWAY?

I was only five years old when my granddad first took me to Saint James' Park, the home of Newcastle United Football Club. After winning the FA Cup three times in five years, the side were on the wane, but they still played in the First Division of the Football League and home games were very entertaining with plenty of goals. I loved every minute of it, the colour, the roar of the fiercely partisan crowd and the excitement when United scored was electric – I was hooked.

I can only just remember Jackie Milburn, the greatest hero in the club's illustrious history. An imposingly large bronze statue of Jackie now stands outside the stadium where he thrilled the fans for over two decades. When he passed away a few years ago, the citizens of Newcastle turned out in their thousands to pay tribute to a wonderful player and also a great man. But I was too young to have witnessed his best years; I had to make do with years of mediocrity as the club slid into decline, resulting in 1961 in relegation to the old Division Two, renamed 'The Championship' these days. They bounced back after four years, so in virtually all my time at the school United played in the top echelon even if success was a bit thin on the ground.

Not everyone at school followed the 'Magpies', which is Newcastle United's nickname since they play in black-and-white stripes. To my surprise, some kids had no interest in football at all. Those who liked the game but didn't follow the local side were often loners, who claimed to support far-away sides like Manchester United, just as many still do up and down the country. Worst of all, though, were the Sunderland fans.

There were only about fifty or so of them in the whole school, but the boy Sting could be counted among their hideous ranks. For some strange reason, Wallsend, where he grew up, has always contained these degenerates in its population. Being firmly embedded on the banks of the Tyne, Wallsend is nowhere near Sunderland, so it always puzzled me why so many of Wallsend's young men supported a team some 14 miles away when a much better club was sitting on their doorstep. Perhaps it is a perverted way of asserting individuality. Whatever the reason, Sting pinned his colours to a red-and-white mast. I blamed a pal of Sting's for his perversion: Peter Keeler was a devoted Sunderland fan from the same Wallsend junior school as

Sting, St Columba's. He went to all their matches, home and away, and I think he brainwashed Sting into joining him in his delusion. 'Leek', as Peter was known to all and sundry, and Sting were my best pals in our first year. So long as we kept the football rivalry off the agenda, we got along just fine.

The only times we fell out were when Newcastle played Sunderland and we could no longer keep our allegiances to ourselves. We niggled at each other continually. I took some of Leek's textbooks home and put black-and-white covers on them, while Leek wrote 'Black and White Shite' on the back of my haversack.

The actual results of the derby matches tended to even out over time. We won our home matches and they won theirs, with the odd draw interspersed; neither side ever seemed to get well hammered. The rivalry at school was mainly good-natured, but, at the matches themselves, it was different. Opposing sets of supporters met head-on in violent tribal confrontations inside and outside the grounds. Often there were hundreds of arrests at matches where attendances regularly topped 50,000.

It was obvious to his Newcastle-supporter friends that Sting was not the dyed-in-the-wool Sunderland fan that his mate Leek was. After a Sunderland defeat (even against Newcastle), Sting didn't appear to be too concerned, whereas Leek would go absent for days with a mysterious illness rather than face the scorn he would get at school. As almost all his other mates were United fans, we decided to try and convert Sting to the way of righteousness. We would convert him... using physical persuasion if necessary.

As 1968 came to a close, Newcastle were on a good run. The previous season, by some miracle United had qualified to play in their first European competition, the Inter-Cities Fairs Cup, now named the UEFA Cup. Playing in front of 55,000 fanatics, we had knocked out such famous sides as Feyenoord of Holland, Sporting Lisbon from Portugal and Spain's Real Zaragoza. The fans were on Cloud Nine as the 'Toon' marched towards the final. We had originally invited Sting along to one of the matches as an independent observer, but once there he quickly joined in with our baying and chanting as we sent Vittoria Setubal crashing out of the competition at the quarter-final stage. The home leg, played during a snowstorm on Tyneside in February, resulted in a 5–1 win for the 'Bonny Lads'. Some of the Portuguese players had never seen snow before, let alone played on it. They had no chance.

The draw for the semi-final matched Newcastle against the cream of Scotland, Glasgow Rangers – a game all of Tyneside and half of Clydeside wanted to see. Sting, in the throes of mid-conversion, chose to go to the home leg without any coercion. The transfer of his loyalties – though he still insisted he also wanted Sunderland to do well – was almost complete. Our own feelings towards the red-and-white scarecrows were summed up in a simple ditty sung to the tune of the 'Grand Old Duke of York':

'There was the Leazes End, they had ten
thousand men,
They marched them up to Roker Park,
And fucked the Fulwell End.'

The second verse was a bit like the first.

'There was the Fulwell End, they had two
thousand men,
They marched them up to St James' Park,
And were never seen again.'

Along with the rest of us, Sting queued for hours before getting a ticket for the Rangers game. Come the day of the match, which was being played on a Wednesday night, the atmosphere at school was charged with electricity. United had drawn the away leg at Ibrox Park 0–0 and Newcastle's goalie, Ian McFaul, had saved an Andy Penman penalty, so a win at St James' would send us into the final.

That Wednesday, we had a half-day which gave us plenty of time to go home, eat, festoon ourselves in black and white, then have a couple of pints before the little matter of the semi-final tie. After school, however, the day did not go entirely to plan.

In those days, the main road from Glasgow to Newcastle ran right past the school gates. Since early on in the day, coaches carrying Rangers fans had been trundling past. These visitors could not have helped noticing a large sign, proclaiming, 'Saint Cuthbert's Roman Catholic Grammar School'.

Rangers supporters, Protestant to a man and narrowly sectarian in outlook, were seen giving 'the fingers' to some of the departing pupils. When we seniors left, we saw a big, white cloth had been draped over the school sign. It bore the legend: '1690 GERS RULE OK F.T.P.'.

Not many of us understood the wording. Most of us worked out the 'Gers RULE OK' bit, but '1690' and 'F.T.P.' were puzzling. Sting, a history student on the quiet, informed the group that 1690 referred to the Battle of the Boyne, where the Protestant William of Orange defeated King James II's Catholic army. 'F.T.P.' was an abbreviated insult to Catholics; it stood for 'Fuck the Pope'.

After Sting's learned explanation, the boys hauled down the banner. After they had jumped up and down on it for a while, some pyromaniac set fire to it. It was particularly bad timing as a Rangers coach was passing by the school at the time and its occupants took exception to the ceremonial burning.

The bus stopped and several boozed-up Jocks alighted to confront the boys. At their approach, most of us – Sting and I included – took off at a rate of knots. Some of the younger kids still coming out of the school fell into the clutches of the tartan nutters. They were in the process of getting a good hiding, when our conscience got the better of us and we decided to return to fight the foe, knowing we would probably get the same treatment.

We were no heroes, but we really couldn't let these poor

little sods get a thrashing. Happily, the cavalry was at hand. Some of the staff were leaving and witnessed the fracas. Peter Barron, the Geography master, a prop-forward with build to match, fearlessly confronted the enemy. Another master, Mr Snowdon, helped us out as well. Barron, who looked made to play the part, was awesome in his defence of the school and Catholicism. When more Rangers fans got off the bus to join in, an outbreak of serious public disorder threatened. Older pupils joined the scene, as well as some more masters. Sting and I watched closely but stayed out of it as we were clearly winning the day. Eventually, the Rangers fans retreated to the safety of their coach, bowed and beaten.

The Battle of Westgate Hill had been won by the Catholic troops of St Cuthbert's – Commanding Officer, General Sir Peter Barron VC – the Boyne had been avenged.

In a turgid match at St James' – where the Rangers supporters invaded the pitch, no doubt in retaliation for their earlier thrashing – United emerged victorious, just as the school had. We won 2–0. In our first venture into European football, we had reached the final. As the history books record, we went on to win the trophy, 6–2 on aggregate, against Ujpest Dosza of Hungary. The cup was ours! We drank, we cried, we sang, we drank some more. Sting was a born-again Magpie and all was right with the world.

The day after the Rangers match, when Sting and I approached the school before lessons, there was a huge

white banner again draped over the school sign. This
time, it read: '1969 GERS RUE K.O. H.T.L.'. What did
the 'H.T.L.' mean? 'HA'WAY THE LADS'. What else!

25 – EE-AYE-ADDIO, WE WOUND THE CUP

Few days were as good as the day we beat Rangers in the semi-final, but there was one day which was just as confrontational and exciting. It was when the St Cuthbert's First XI won the National Schools Football Trophy. Since the very first team was picked at St Cuthbert's in our first year, I had been a regular member of the school team. However, in my final year, my appearances in the First XI were restricted to only a couple of outings due to the outstanding form shown by Phil Atkinson, a lad two years younger than me who had forced his way into the side.

Sting, although a good athlete, was useless at playing with a round ball. He was usually restricted to playing with the fatties and the kids who looked like they had their legs on back to front. Despite Sting's inability to trap the ball with the sole of the foot, never mind the knees, he has been a lifelong follower of the game.

In the first leg of the final played on Tyneside, Sting and I watched our lads run out 2–0 winners against St Michael's, Leeds – Phil Atkinson and Micky Connon were the goal-scorers. A week later, we went to Leeds to support the team in the return leg.

Before the match began, some of the younger St Cuthbert's kids, sitting in the grandstand near Sting and I, rose to the baiting of the home fans and hurled insults back at them. A fracas ensued. Some older Leeds boys cuffed the young lads round the ears. We were getting used to this sort of thing. Much as we hated the idea of physical violence, Sting and I were drawn into the melee. We sorely missed the presence of our pal, Dek Hornsby, who could mix it with the best of them. Neither Sting nor I was noted for our pugilistic skills.

As the punch-up neared us, suddenly a flying fist shot out of the melee and landed squarely on Sting's nose. The thought of losing his good looks through a broken nose spurred the lad into retaliatory action. He waded into the Leeds' thugs with relish. Looking like a boxing kangaroo, head well back to avoid further damage, his fists whirred around like lawnmower blades. Things eventually calmed down and, having settled matters to his satisfaction, he sat back down in his seat wiping his hands.

'Right, I've done my bit,' he said with aplomb. 'Now it's time for those tossers on the pitch to do theirs.'

The game was going according to plan, namely to

hold on to our 2–0 lead, when Joe Bulman scored for us, increasing our advantage to three goals. Now, surely the outcome would be a formality. Unbelievably, the dreaded complacency crept in and, before we knew it, Leeds had scored twice. At 3–2, everything was back in the melting pot. Not for the first time, our team captain sent the proceedings into the realms of the ridiculous. Hughie McBride headed the ball away after a corner, then suddenly stopped in his tracks. He slapped his hand to his temple and asked for the referee to halt the game. The plonker had lost one of his contact lenses! Both sides scoured the muddy pitch for what seemed like an hour in a vain attempt to find the tiny lens. The game restarted with Hughie, a swivel-eyed git at the best of times, now almost blind according to legal definition.

Within seconds of the resumption, in his stupor Hughie gave away a penalty that was converted to make the score 3–3 on aggregate.

With only minutes left to play, extra-time beckoned. Due to the long delay caused by Hughie's lens search, and in the absence of floodlighting, it was almost dark. As the game could not be continued past 90 minutes, the officials decided that the trophy should be shared between the two school sides. Sting suggested that we played them at pontoon for the outright honour, but a toss of a coin was enough to give us the trophy for the first six months. Hughie's correct call of 'Heads' was the signal for the St Cuthbert's contingent to take a lap of honour. We ran on to the pitch, hoisted our blind captain on to our shoulders and paraded him and the cup around the ground to a crescendo of booing from the home fans, which we acknowledged by giving them the fingers. Who said sportsmanship was dead?

Relinquishing a three-goal advantage did not detract from the exuberant celebrations on our return to Newcastle. That evening we adjourned to the Durham Ox pub in the city. It was Sting's inspired idea to fill the cup with champagne. A whip-round only raised the sum of three pounds twelve and two pence (£3.61), so we settled for Newcastle Brown Ale. That was a big mistake as Sting and I had earlier experiences with this potent brew and we had come off second best.

Not surprisingly, things started to get out of hand. The overflowing cup, at first limited to the St Cuthbert's party, had been commandeered by some of the tough Durham Ox regulars. They were all enjoying a free swallow and, while it still contained beer, they were none too keen to hand it back.

After his victory earlier in the day, Sting was the automatic choice to attempt to retrieve the trophy from the freeloaders. The cup may have been in mortal danger of ending up on a stranger's mantelpiece but Sting was in no fit state to tackle anyone. The surfeit of Brown Ale had rendered him incapable. Hughie was the next choice to ask politely for the safe return of the hard-won cup from its new holders. Still blind as a bat, he appeared to be addressing the wall when he shouted, 'If you don't give us back that fucking cup now, the boys will kick the shit out of you!' mistakenly pointing to two old soaks standing at the bar.

The new cup-holders fell about laughing, before kindly flinging the silverware at him. It bounced off the skipper's head and crashed to the floor. We quickly scooped it up and were out of the door in a flash. Just when we thought we were safe, tragedy struck. Sting had taken hold of the cup and, in time-honoured fashion, was balancing it on his head. It hadn't been there for more than three seconds when he keeled over and sent it crashing to the pavement. Hughie, who could only make out vague outlines, went over to pick Sting up, only to tread on the trophy with his size-11 boots. The cup buckled under his weight.

Hughie inspected the damage, holding it up close to his nose to see it. He let out an anguished roar of pain. 'It's fucked!' he cried. 'The fucking cup's fucking fucked!' Sting and I collapsed to the ground doubled up with laughter, as Hughie smashed at the trophy with his fist in a predictably unsuccessful attempt to get it back in shape. Sympathetically, we howled in his face before staggering off into the night in search of the nearest fish and chip shop – the compulsory routine for drunks when the pubs close.

On entering the steamy chippy, we were faced by the mob that had tried to wrest the cup from our grasp in the Durham Ox. When they saw its current state, they just sneered in contempt. One of them said, 'We don't want it now it's been run over by a steamroller.'

After consuming a disgusting mound of congealed,

greasy chips, we reflected on our predicament. The boss was due to present the cup to Hughie at assembly on Monday morning. It could not be allowed to get to him in this state – we would all be shot.

Ludicrously, we decided that all we could do was take a bloody big hammer to it and try and thrash it back into the shape of the National Schools trophy. It was going to be quite a task and not one to be undertaken in our present state of inebriation.

It was nearly midnight and, in order to keep up the conspiracy, we decided to spend the night at my house in Longbenton. The all-night bus for the East End of Newcastle was due, so we headed for the bus stop near to Newcastle Central Station. As might be expected, these buses were patronised almost exclusively by drunks and lunatics. Tonight we qualified on both counts. By journey's end, I had won an army greatcoat in a game of poker, Sting was engaged to be married to a lesbian and Hughie had been offered a job as a window-cleaner in Kuala Lumpur, a prospect which excited him greatly.

On Sunday morning, unsurprisingly, we were badly hungover, a condition made worse when we clapped eyes on the cup for the first time as sober men. It was battered beyond recognition. I asked my dad for his very finest hammer, which he reluctantly handed over when I told him of our bizarre plight. St Cuthbert's was an old-fashioned grammar school and we were totally untested in the manual skills needed for metal or woodwork; Latin was more up our street.

Sting gleefully volunteered to salvage the twisted bit of silverware. He went at it like a man possessed, slamming the hammer into the cup with ever-increasing force. At each new blow, I expected the cup to disintegrate as Hughie and I held on as firmly as possible. In our ignorance, my dad's vice stood unused at our elbows. After crashing and banging away for twenty minutes, Sting had done a surprisingly good job. The cup looked something like a cup again.

When Monday morning came, the boss handed the cup over to Hughie in front of the whole school, none the wiser about the artisan Sting's handiwork. If he ever packs up the music business, I'm sure he will have no difficulty in getting a job down the shipyards. Just quote Hughie and me as referees, Sting.

26 – BEATLEMANIA – HAIR TODAY, GONE TOMORROW

Considering the success that Sting has achieved as a musician, songwriter and, unbelievably, as a singer, he was not all that musically inclined as a schoolboy. The music lessons we had consisted almost entirely of singing – a reasonable education for football fans, but no more.

A few kids were encouraged to play musical instruments; our mate, Trevor Dyson, played the trumpet for instance. He was so bad that his neighbours reported him to the police for strangling geese in his bedroom. Sting, who could not even make the school choir, messed about on guitar; he'd been encouraged to play more by listening to Cream's Jack Bruce than by any formal teaching at the school.

During our years at St Cuthbert's, a musical revolution was taking place with the advent of Merseybeat and the emergence of the Beatles. Sting was a big Beatles fan and their music had a great effect on his early development as a budding musician and songwriter. Sting also liked the Rolling Stones but I never shared his passion where they were concerned. I contented myself with being a devoted Beatles fan.

I decorated my haversack with a large tribute to the group. It read simply 'THE BEATLES' in bold, black felt-tip pen. I drew four beetles around this inscription and was very pleased with my efforts until I overheard some kids remark that, for some strange reason, I had drawn four mice on the back of my bag. When I looked more closely, they had a point. My beetles only had four legs, so I added a couple more. The result of the improvement was that those same kids now asked why I had centipedes on my bag.

Defeated, I blacked them out, transforming them into large musical notes. The comments continued. I heard a fifth-year sneeringly comment, 'Christ, look at fucking Mozart's haversack.' I finally deleted my tribute altogether, painted it over and settled for 'Newcastle United'. The wisecracks soon stopped.

Over the first few years of our incarceration in St Cuthbert's, the fervour Sting and I had for the Beatles never wavered. Then the big day arrived when the news we had been waiting to hear for so long arrived: the Beatles were coming to Newcastle. They were appearing in concert at Newcastle City Hall. The chances of actually getting a ticket for the concert were fairly remote but we did try. The day the tickets went on sale,

Sting and I took an illicit day off school, arriving at the City Hall box office at the crack of dawn only to discover that fans had been queuing there for three or four days. At the front of the queue, some people had tents with beds and cooking equipment; others had deckchairs and sun-loungers!

We trudged around the corner to see lines of fans disappearing into the distance. We couldn't believe our eyes; we thought we were fans! These people were in a different class. After languishing at the back of the never-ending snake of followers for a couple of hours, we were told that all the tickets had been sold. We buggered off home, sick as a nudist in a nettle bed. We did vow, though, that we would still turn out on the night of the concert, if only to sample the atmosphere and perhaps catch a glimpse of our heroes.

At school, many of the pupils had entered into the spirit of things by sporting Beatle haircuts, while others turned their blazer lapels inside out in imitation of Beatle jackets. At school on the day of the concert, excitement was at fever pitch – though many pupils boasted they had tickets, none was produced as proof. Sting and I met up in Newcastle's Haymarket a good two hours before the concert was due to start. We watched in a fit of jealousy as ticket-holders waved their prizes in celebration. These were people who owned camping gear fit for an assault on Everest and could apparently take a week off work.

As we neared the venue, we joined a throng of like-minded fans. By a gargantuan effort, considering we were nowhere near the front of the heaving masses gathered around the tiny stage door, we managed to inch forward. With much pushing, shoving and cursing, and despite fierce opposition, we almost got to the front by the stage door. In the distance we could hear screams from the fans. The noise rose to a crescendo as the crowd around us got caught up in the hysteria.

The 'Fab Four' were getting nearer, a signal for me to contribute to the clamour. I let rip, 'Paul, Paul!' I hollered for no reason other than the fact that most of the others were doing likewise. I had thought that the vast majority of the screaming hordes would be young girls but, as it turned out, there were just as many young lads in the crowd. I was a little concerned I would be labelled a 'poof', but, as some of the lads were really tough-looking, my fears were allayed.

But, of the two sexes, the girls were even more determined to reach the Liverpool lads. Their fanatical desire to touch their idols was as desperate as it was frightening at close quarters. The Beatles climbed from their limos, as their burly minders cleared a way through the swaying mass of fans for them to get safely inside the hall. Their appearance was the catalyst for scenes of total chaos.

John Lennon was the first to battle his way through the mob; he passed by only inches from me. Some ultra-determined fans hurled themselves forward in a vain attempt to touch him. As the crowd closed in,

George Harrison followed. The crush was so great now it was in danger of producing casualties. I was right in the firing line due to some ferocious pushing from behind by frantic girls, who were now becoming as worried about the dangers of overcrowding as they had previously been about not getting to touch the group.

Then it was Paul McCartney's turn to force his way past. Paul had always been the most popular of the Beatles with teenage girls and his presence caused the greatest crowd congestion yet. Almost gasping for breath, I was pushed right up on him for a second. Minutes earlier I had been calling his name, but now that had lost its appeal. I was too weak at this point and blaring his name in his face, like others were doing, seemed silly in the extreme. It was as if the effect of a strange drug had suddenly worn off on me. He was just a man after all, albeit a very famous one.

While I was standing amid this massive condensed sea of humanity trying to regain my breath and my sanity, some idiot grabbed me, presumably in a mistimed attempt to grab Paul. Thinking that they had touched their idol's precious locks, they took a handful – not of Paul's hair, but of mine! We had been that close together. My state of high excitement was rapidly disappearing.

Ringo Starr was the last of the quartet to fumble his way through the melee. Again I became almost jammed against the object of the crowd's enthusiasm. As all around cried, 'Ringo, Ringo,' the only words I could think of uttering were 'Jesus, what a hooter!' Not used to abuse from fans, Ringo flashed me a not-too-appreciative glance, but he was quickly ushered away.

With the group now safely inside the City Hall, the crowd rapidly dispersed, some to see the concert and many more to gather round the front of the building. It was rumoured that the band played so loudly that they could be heard in the street. I spotted Sting looking decidedly dishevelled, moving gingerly towards the front of the house. We met up to test the rumour that we were about to enjoy a free concert. All we could hear, though, was the screaming audience. After a couple of minutes of that, we had had enough. We headed for home.

As we were about to part, Sting solemnly announced that he had something of great importance to tell me. I listened with bated breath as he informed me that, when Paul McCartney had passed us, he had lost his balance in a massive surge forward. He reached out to save himself and in the confusion grabbed a handful of Paul's hair. He opened his grubby paw to reveal a few strands of dark hair, my hair! The silly sod thought that it was from the head of his hero. I didn't have the heart to disappoint him and tell him where it had really come from.

At school, he showed everyone my hair, even keeping his trophy in a silver snuffbox for a while. I don't suppose Sting has it any more and I'm sorry if I have shattered any illusions that it was Paul's in the first place. Should he ever want to replace it, he need only ask.

Maybe if he wanted to get hold of the real thing he

could ask Paul for a swap. The trouble is, these days Sting no longer has much hair to chuck around. I do not look forward to the sight of Sting looking like a boiled egg but, in all honesty, he is well on his way to just that.

27 – BOB'S FULL HOUSE

Our all-boys Catholic Grammar School hardly gave us an ideal grounding in the skills of chatting up girls, if we ever got to meet any in the first place. Those of us without either older sisters or next-door neighbours with teenage daughters virtually never met girls of our own age.

Our growing awareness of the attractions of womankind coincided with our developing a taste for the hop. Although Sting was often the first to suggest a piss-up, he wasn't much of a boozer himself. Being tall, blond and relatively handsome – or at least he was by comparison with the rest of us – he should have been a wow with the girls. But he was too introverted at the time to notice that some girls did, in fact, fancy him.

Like the rest of us, he had more experience of getting pissed than getting laid. Newcastle Brown Ale had got the better of him twice. His last confrontation with 'lunatic's broth' had seen him go home, enter the living room where his parents were watching TV and proclaim himself unhappy with the reception. He then proceeded to try and take the back off the set before being ushered away to bed by his dad. After this encounter, he decided that 'Broon' was not his tipple after all.

Nevertheless, he never missed a social opportunity. We mistakenly believed that by visiting the pubs and clubs of the area we would meet young girls of similar persuasion. Only when we started frequenting jazz clubs like the Club A Go-Go did anyone have any success and that was to be a couple of years in the future. In those days, girls of our age did not go into pubs, though it took us long enough for this to dawn on us. Our search for the opposite sex was never going to meet with success if we continued to go to the Post Office Bar and the Printer's Pie, our two favourite drinking haunts. They were very male-oriented pubs. No woman under the age of sixty would be seen dead in them.

Bob Taylor, one of our drinking partners, told us that his parents were going on holiday and they were leaving him in charge of the family home, a nice semi in Tynemouth. On the first Saturday night of his parents' holiday, Bob was throwing a party at the house.

It was a select bunch that was invited to Bob's party that Saturday night – the usual crew: Sting, me, Hughie, Tony, Joe, Trevor, Paul and Alan Sutherland. Alan, was, and still is, a friend of mine from Longbenton. I have known him all my life. He knew Sting and the rest of the lads from our visits to the Printer's Pie. There was a slight problem with Alan, however. It wasn't the fact that he didn't attend St Cuthbert's or the fact that he was, shamefully, a civil servant. It was simple religious bigotry. He was a non-Catholic. As only a couple of us were practising Catholics – in particular Joe, who had been a kick-in-the-arse off becoming a priest – we hypocritically decided beforehand that we would convert Alan to Catholicism, by force if necessary.

To his credit, Bob had tried to find some girls to join the sex-starved gang. We had completely left it up to him to invite over twenty nubile nymphomaniacs but he had managed to coax just two young lasses to the party. Bob turned out to be as useless as the rest of us, who couldn't score with an Essex girl in a lift stuck between floors. Still it was a good mix: eight lads and two girls.

Bob himself and the neurotic Sting had first crack at the two lovelies. The rest of us moped around, sinking vast quantities of lager and watching with brooding menace as the foursome smooched around the living-room floor to Leonard Cohen. Trev went out to slit his wrists. Meanwhile, the likely lads danced on for a while until the comments about their personal habits, hygiene and shortcomings in the trouser department had the desired effect and they gave up the chase. Joe and Tony took up the gauntlet, until it was decided it was time for 'the Christening'.

The conspirators sidled over to Alan and began by

casually asking him if he had ever wanted to embrace the true faith. He answered in the negative, citing his reasons as being his horror at the thought of confession – he didn't fancy telling a stranger about his solitary sex life; his 'one-in-a-bed' sex romps were private. Even worse than that, he argued, was his fear of having ashes smudged on his forehead, which Sting had told him must not be washed off on pain of death. We put him at his ease. He shouldn't have any fear about telling strangers he was a wanker; had he not just done so without a hint of embarrassment or recrimination? The ashes business was only on Ash Wednesday and it would only look like he had finished a round on the bins. You 'could' wash it off, anyway – albeit a week later while keeping your fingers crossed, one foot off the ground and whistling 'Faith of Our Fathers'.

Alan's reasons for remaining a Protestant were not considered significant enough to stop the enforced conversion. We commenced the baptism. I held Alan by the head, while Hughie poured gallons of water over his curly bonce and Sting claimed his soul from the Devil. He was asked to pay £2 in administration costs for the privilege. At one point Hughie had slightly 'oversaturated' the lad who began gulping for breath. Bob pulled his head from the sink in time to stop the first-ever death while being baptised. Luckily for Alan, he would have gone straight to Heaven as he was now in a state of grace.

Before the fun began, Bob had told us that two

instructions must be strictly obeyed. We could, he said, drink every drop of liquid in the place, including the contents of the fish-tank, with one exception: we were not to go anywhere near his father's pride and joy, a 12-year-old Irish malt whiskey. We were also told that we were permitted to misuse any item of furniture, except for the chess table, which was antique, irreplaceable and beyond value in money and sentiment. We readily agreed. None of us was a spirit drinker and, boring though this party might be, we didn't think a game of chess would enliven proceedings. If things fizzled out, we could have some fun teaching Alan the responses in the Latin mass.

No one was remotely interested in the malt or the chess table, so when neither of them was around in less than five minutes flat, it had obviously taken a gargantuan effort by someone. Cometh the hour, cometh the man: Sting had been brooding ever since his failure with the girls. Getting progressively more drunk, he was flinging lager after lager down his throat. I was standing at the bottom of the stairs, arguing with Alan about the Pope's infallibility. 'Then why doesn't he do the fucking pools, then?' was his heretical response. Baptised and excommunicated on the same day. Some achievement!

Sting pushed past me on the stairs, avoiding tracer-fire judging by his zigzag course. Only when he was at the top did I realise that he had a whiskey bottle in his hand – *the* whiskey bottle! He shouted down at me, 'How, Berryman! I bet you a fiver, I can slide down the banister.' Without waiting for confirmation of the wager, he was away. He shot down the banister, which must surely have been coated in goose grease if his velocity at take-off was to be believed. On reaching the bottom, he flew through the air like a pissed ski-jumper. Still holding the whiskey bottle, he landed slap-bang on top of the chess table, smashing it into matchwood. The malt bottle disintegrated when it hit the polished wooden floor. The demise of the prized objects, although tragic, somehow had a poetic inevitability...

Bob stood transfixed as his life flashed before his eyes. Sting was apologetic and offered to pay for the damage. Bob just gave out the maniacal laugh of the damned. We replaced the malt but Bob's dad never did get the chance to take his prized possession to *The Antiques Road Show*. The whiskey bottle debacle should have been curtains for the party, but if anything events got even more out of hand. A violent game of two-a-side football broke out in the garage. The noise emanating from here – ball banging against the walls, screams of pain and expletives aplenty – was enough for the neighbours to call the police. It was only 2.00am. Some people just won't let you have fun. The girls were long-gone and Bob had turned into a shambolic figure, whimpering about death and destruction.

New Catholic Alan spotted two tricycles in the garage. He mounted one of them and challenged all-comers to a race up the street on the other bike. Only Sting took up the gauntlet. After much gambling on the outcome, they were off. Racing out of Bob's street, they were soon on a main road. Their legs, alcohol propelled, whizzed round.

They seemed to be doing about 30 miles an hour in a thrilling, if dangerous, head to head. The same coppers, who had been to the house about the noise, apprehended the boy-racers. Sting later claimed that they were done for speeding, while Alan said they were arrested for being drunk in charge of a deadly weapon. Whatever the charges had been, they were dropped and soon they were back in the house and back on the sauce.

With the drink running out and the house resembling a battlefield, we were required to fight for the right to one of the beds. Sting and I won the honour to share a double bed. After a couple of hours' kip, Sting threatened to kill me. He claimed, quite falsely I believe, that I could snore for Britain – I had only just broken into the county side; I would never represent my country. He swore he would never sleep with me again. To be fair, he has kept his promise.

As if things weren't bad enough, Sting and Hughie decided to greet the sunrise by howling out an appalling dirge, 'Since my baby left me, I ain't got no place to go…' they chanted. I don't know if this was a real song or whether, as seemed likely by its extreme tunelessness, Sting had made it up. Whatever the verdict, I swore, if I had the strength, I would get up and murder the pair of bastards. Little did I know then, but I would have to listen to endless versions of 'Since My Baby Left Me' over the next thirty years, belted out by the wailing Sting. If only I had had the sense of purpose to climb from that bed and kill him that morning, the world might have been a better place. But I didn't and it isn't.

28 – FROM THE CANARIES TO A DOG'S LIFE

'The best years of your life' is how someone once described school days. This statement is a load of bollocks, unless you substitute the word 'worst' for 'best'. None of my pals at school enjoyed their time there. You could tell by the looks on their faces before and after the school day. They would file through the gates at 9.00am as if they were about to face a firing squad. At 4.00pm, jubilation abounded as they playfully scampered away again, only for the process to be repeated the following day. My demeanour was exactly the same as my pals... manically depressed. Friday night was like New Year's Eve. Goodwill flowed after another week at the mill had bitten the dust. The atmosphere immediately before the end of term was terrific. Kids who hadn't spoken to you all term suddenly wanted to be your best pal. Even the masters cheered up and starting telling jokes, probably out of relief at their impending escape. The holidays were always over much too quickly, while term-time lasted longer than a thousand requiem masses. I loved every second of the long summer recess and treasured its arrival as much as I mourned its departure from one year to the next.

Despite our shared hatred of the daily slog along the West Road, great friendships were formed at the school. In our shared adversity, we swore allegiance to each other until the time of our release and, in a lot of cases, for many years to come. In our early teens, the summer hols were one long game of football or cricket and we lapped it up. In late-teens, things changed and not necessarily for the better. Totally unreasonably, parents decided that, now you were old enough to shave and drink beer, you were no longer worthy of the luxury of a holiday; you were expected to take summer jobs. Apparently, it was not enough for you to have worked your nuts off studying for examinations; now you were expected to earn a crust as well.

Some of the boys already did part-time work – paper rounds and so on – which they carried out both before and after school. Masochists, I imagined. Judging by the colour of their hands, some kids had just worked the early shift down the local pit. I swear that one of the first-years was either a chimney sweep or the sweep used the kid's head as a brush. He had black dandruff for Christ's sake! Sting often worked for his dad on his milk round, so working the holidays wasn't the horror that it was for some of his contemporaries.

In our first year as sixth-formers, Sting went on holiday with Hughie to Ireland. They came back with wild tales of the 'Troubles', but as they were Geordies most of the locals thought they were as hard as nails. At a party they got invited to, such was their reputation that they were asked to act as bouncers for a while. They even did some work while they were there. They were extras on the film *Ryan's Daughter*, starring the Oscar-winning Sir John Mills, Robert Mitchum and Sarah Miles. It is probably the only decent film Sting has ever been associated with, I reckon. I managed to skive through those holidays without having to resort to labour but it also meant I was too poor to go with Sting and Hughie to Ireland. A year later, my luck finally ran out.

My mother found me a job in a warehouse in Byker, one of the roughest areas in the East End of Newcastle. The owner, Mr George Logan, often frequented Brough Park for the greyhound racing. My mam worked in the restaurant there, hence the connection and the offer of the job. He told my mam there might be two vacancies for smart boys and added that if I knew of anyone else interested I should let him know. I asked all my pals but received a series of blank stares in reply. The wages of £1-a-day might just have had a teeny-weeny effect on their enthusiasm. I was going to have to face the mean streets of Byker alone.

I needed a plan in order to be accepted into the ranks

of tough Byker warehousemen. I decided to dress as shabbily as possible, not wash my hair for a fortnight and vowed to curse after every other word that I uttered. That should do, I thought.

I only had one more day to enjoy before my life as a working man started, so I went into town to have a drink with Sting. When I saw him, he was almost unrecognisable from the lad I saw at school each day. His hair flowed down his back, several days' growth of wispy beard stood out on his chin and he wore psychedelic bell-bottomed trousers with a skimpy waistcoat that exposed his midriff. I told him that he looked like a refugee. He was well chuffed. He looked as though he was enjoying life and he soon told me why. Hughie had written to him to tell him that he had found both of them a job in the Canaries. They were to start the following Monday and work lasted until we were due back at school. Hughie hadn't said what the job was, but Sting reckoned it would be in a club or bar, or even as a lifeguard. The money wasn't that great but the thought of the sun and sex was overwhelming. Hughie, he said, had really come up trumps this time.

I stood and listened to him in a state of clinical shock. Those two bastards were going to have the time of their lives in the Canaries, while I languished in a Byker craphole. I was almost too upset to speak but I managed to tell Sting that, when I met up with Hughie again, I would be armed and dangerous. He could have got me a job there as well surely?

After a brief pint, which went down like ink, I walked away from Sting as if all the camel shit in the Sahara had landed on my shoulders. I thought I only got depressed at school but this was worse. The thought of those two sunning themselves, drinking and fornicating, while I lugged heavy boxes around in a midden, was a living nightmare. I decided I would start my working life in the manner in which I intended to continue – I would have a week on the sick!

My mother was none too pleased with the mystery ailment that had consumed me, but, as I never left my bed for a week, she was at least convinced something was wrong. When she insisted I saw the doctor, I got up to face my responsibilities. I would commence my duties as a warehouse technician on the Monday.

I had the weekend to myself. On Saturday morning I went into Newcastle in search of succour. I met a sucker. I spotted Sting who was supposed to be abroad. I knew it was him from fifty paces. No one in Newcastle dressed like that. I grabbed him by the shoulders, wheeling him away from the shop window he was aimlessly gazing into. 'What the frigging hell are you doing here? I thought you were in the Canaries. Sand, sex, sangria, sunstroke etcetera. Why are you still here?' I asked, feigning concern.

He gave me a pained look. 'Me and Hughie have been to Bradford for four days,' Sting replied edgily.

'Bradford? Is there a place called "Bradford" in the Canaries?' I asked.

'Not as far as I know,' he went on. 'But there is a fucking cannery in Bradford!'

'I'm a bit confused. Would you care to elaborate?' I asked, now warming to his tale of woe.

He took a deep breath and spat it out. 'You know that Hughie wrote to me telling me he had found us jobs in the Canaries? Well, his fucking spelling is shite. He meant to write that he had got us jobs in the "canneries". A fucking canning plant! In bastard Bradford! I had to go. I was totally broke. My dad has even taken on a new kid on the milk. I'm up shit creek!'

I should have laughed in his face, as he surely would have done to me. I settled for a broad grin.

He continued to moan. 'I could only stand the place for a couple of days. Look at my hands! Much more of that and I might never play the guitar again.'

'So some good might come out of it then?' I teased, biting my lip so hard I felt a trickle of blood in my mouth. Only someone with a heart of stone would not have broken down in hysterics. Proving the merit of my vital organ, I burst into a torrent of guffawing.

He never could take a joke and turned to walk away. But he stopped in his tracks when I shouted after him, 'I might be able to help you get a job, if you can be arsed!'

He asked what it was.

'If you still want a job, there's one at this warehouse place, the House of Logan. It's not much dosh but we'll have a laugh. I'm pretty sure you can start the same day as me, this coming Monday.'

'OK. Tell me where it is and I'll see you Monday morning, bright and early,' Sting demanded.

I told him what he wanted to know, then we went for a drink in the Monkey Bar in Newcastle. We listened to Thunderclap Newman's hit 'Something in the Air' belting out from the pub's jukebox. This turned out to be a very apt song because, on that Sunday in July 1969, man was about to set foot on the moon for the first time. Neil Armstrong, a Geordie if his name was anything to go by, would make his 'giant step for mankind' as the whole of the western world watched on in awe. I would be asking Sting what he thought about this event on the morrow, our first depressing day as trainee warehousemen.

29 – DONE UP LIKE A DOG'S BREAKFAST

I ambled up to the House of Logan the day after the moon landing. The work force was lounging outside, moaning. I heard one of them say, 'Did you see all that moon-shite last night? What a load of cobblers!'

'Aye, you're right. It was a reet pile of crap!' another genius agreed. 'Boring as fuck!'

I had never met these two before but I thought that we might be on different wavelengths. I had been captivated by the events of the previous night.

I ambled a bit closer before telling them that my mate and I were starting work there that day. They were infuriated because a couple of the regulars had been laid off the previous week because of lack of work. One insinuated that we must be Mr Logan's relations.

'No, you're wrong there, mate. I've never met the bloke before, ya fucker,' I replied, remembering to swear.

He just ignored me. I told them we were just students with jobs for the holidays. I might just as well have told him that we were child molesters with Sunderland season tickets. The moans got even louder. I wished Sting would hurry up.

The doors flung open and the rabble trundled morosely inside. I was about to go through the door when a hand grasped my shoulder and stopped me in my tracks. It was Sting, dressed like he was going for a job in the City. I looked in amazement at his smart suit. He had even had his haircut. He informed me that he had heard from a neighbour that he had a chance of a job in an estate agent's on Shields Road, just around the corner from the warehouse, and was going there for an interview. He therefore didn't think he would be joining me in the depressing world of warehouse technology. I was gutted but, before I could protest, he was off, leaving me to the jackals of Byker, who I feared might greet me on my first day by squirting oven-cleaner on my genitals, before hacking off my pubic hair with a Stanley knife. I had heard about these depraved rituals before.

In the event, nobody spoke to me so I was quite happy. The work was bloody hard, though; there were none of your newfangled forklift trucks to do the lifting here, just many a pair of broad shoulders as wagon after wagon came in to be loaded and unloaded, all with massive amounts of washing powder and other household consumables.

The warehouse itself was an old converted music hall,

which had also once served as a cinema. A ragged old screen still hung at the front on a dilapidated stage and only the seats were missing. It was a weird place. Despite swearing a lot and working as hard as anyone else, I was still an outcast. At the end of the day, I trudged off home, let myself in and promptly fell asleep on top of my sister on our sofa. She couldn't move for three hours with me pinning her down.

When I got up the following day, I felt like I had been run over by a horse and cart during the night. I could barely move my limbs for the first hour, but I managed to struggle back to the warehouse for day two. No one had even mentioned the fact that my partner had not joined me the previous day as apparently it was quite common for new workers to take one look at the place, turn on their heel and leave.

Incredibly, when I arrived at the warehouse that morning, the unlikely figure of Sting was standing in the middle of the work force, while they roared with laughter, slapping him on the back. Considering that they had wanted to disembowel me, I found their affability towards Sting a trifle strange. It turned out he knew nearly all of them as his dad had delivered milk to them for years. His dad, I reckoned, had the biggest bloody milk round in the world. To make things worse, I heard the foreman (another bloody customer of his dad) tell Sting that, as some new dope had started the previous day, he might get him work in the office. Sting looked at the face I was pulling and quickly turned down the offer. He wanted to experience a bit of life.

It was obvious by now that he had failed to get the job at the estate agent's. When he told me why, a shaggy-dog story if ever I heard one, it made me forget where we were for a minute I was so pleased with his dramatic failure.

'I was early for the interview, so I went for a bacon sarnie in a cafe,' he lamented. 'But the tomato ketchup flew out on to my suit trousers. I tried to get it off but there was a big red mark left on the knee. It looked terrible. I walked up Shields Road and this little dog started sniffing at my strides. I know I should have booted it, but it was just a little thing and I thought it might lick the stain clean.'

I looked at him, waiting for the rest of his nonsense, my face betraying no emotion. He continued. 'The fucking thing must have liked the taste, cos it took a big bite at my knee and tore away about ten inches of material. I looked like a bastard scarecrow. I couldn't go to the interview like that. I could only afford a cheap pair of jeans, so I went to an Army and Navy place, got what I thought was the right size and went into the toilets at the top of Shields Road to try them on. They were fucking enormous! Barbar the bastard elephant could have worn them. I didn't have time to go back, so I had to wear them. They had a fifty-inch waist and turn-ups about a fucking foot long. I had to hold the things up with one hand. I went in the estate agent's and the secretary told me the bins were around the back! I eventually saw the manager and he must have thought it was fucking Halloween. I couldn't think of a thing to say when he asked me why I wanted the job, other than I got an hour for lunch. He chucked me out and the jeans fell to my feet when I got up, so I fell flat on my fucking face right at the sexy secretary's feet. I didn't get the job but I've got a date with the secretary, so it wasn't a total disaster,' he finally said.

I had to sit down I was so weak with laughter. Sting just sniffed and went about his day. We spent our next few weeks in that daft place, getting well muscled-up, but one fine day I thought we had lost him in a freak squeaky-toy incident.

30 – ONE SQUEAK FROM YOU AND YOU'RE DEAD!

Under the stage at the front of the converted cinema where the ragged old screen still hung, there was an enormous pit filled with literally thousands of kiddies' squeaky plastic toys. Why they sold them in the first place or how there came to be so many, no one seemed to know or care. The pit was choc-a-bloc with these squeezy dolls, which some of our customers inexplicably bought by the bucketful. Everyone called them 'The Squeaks'. Orders for them were greeted with much disgust since we labourers would be required to climb down into the black dungeon and shovel these hideous things into baskets. Insane people would buy these vile toys in the hope that they could sell them at a profit. One look at them made me feel ill. They leered at you with what can only be described as pure evil. They would have terrified children. I know they terrified Sting and me.

Because we were new boys, any orders for the horrors would be passed on to us. One day, a crazed customer placed an order for twenty baskets. The only explanation we could come up with was that he must have hated a lot of children very much indeed. Management may have been delighted but Sting and I were mortified, especially when it became apparent that it would be our sad task to stuff these monsters into the baskets.

With faces like maggot-farmers, we climbed into the hellhole to start the disinterment. Spades at the ready, we were prepared for a marathon session. To make things even worse, it was rumoured that it wasn't just The Squeaks that lived in the pit but, in the dark recesses where no man had ever been, there were also rats as big as Davy Crockett hats. Sting detested rats so much he could not even say their name, preferring to call them 'longtails'. As I lived in a slightly more affluent district than Wallsend, I couldn't remember ever seeing a rat, but I didn't want to have one biting my arse in this black hole. As Sting reminded me, 'They go for your throat when cornered,' although I was pretty sure he had said the same thing about budgies.

After filling several baskets with The Squeaks, we became aware of scratching noises. We started shovelling even faster, stepping on more and more of the ghastly plastic toys as our digging became more frantic. They squealed louder and louder as I began to pretend that I was stamping them all to death. We were halfway through filling yet another basket, when Sting suddenly yelled, '*A rat*, a fucking rat, I'm outta here!' instantly forgetting the 'longtail' bit.

How he was going to see in the gloom was a mystery. Instead of making for the entrance from which emanated the only dim light in evidence, he made off in the opposite direction in total blind panic.

'Where the fucking hell are you going?' I shouted after him, as he disappeared into the mire where the squeaking horrors were piled up many feet high. They gave out torrents of squeals as he ploughed through them, until his strength failed and he fell among them. These things really did have minds of their own.

The more Sting tried to fight them off, the more they engulfed him. I finally reached him, only to see despite the blackness that he was almost entirely submerged in a sea of squeaking plastic monsters. I shovelled away at them, noticing for the first time that some of them had yellow hair and appeared to be laughing. To my horror, I managed to knock over a massive column of the bastards, which fell and almost knocked both of us unconscious. It was like an episode of *Tales of the Unexpected*; we were slipping into a morass of kitsch terror. We poked our heads out from among The Squeaks, who were clearly pulling us down with their tiny, grasping hands while emitting howls of tinny delight, and shouted as one, 'Help!'

Never mind the rats and what they might do, as our high-pitched captors dragged us under we were almost helpless. Our shouts rose to a scream, until finally help was at hand. John, the most experienced of the workers, whose girlfriend incidentally went by the marvellous name of 'the hunch-back of Pottery Bank', arrived on the scene armed with a massive spade and expertly dug both of us out.

We clambered out happy to have survived the ordeal. All the other labourers seemed to find the incident hilarious. We vowed never to go back in the pit and neither did anyone else as it turned out. That very night, the warehouse was ravaged by fire. The inferno apparently started in the pit, melting down the thousands of inmates who, I imagined, squeaked less and less as they turned into one solid molten mass of burning plastic.

Quite a lot of damage was done especially to the stock but the building remained sound enough. Not surprisingly, Sting and I were at first blamed for the blaze, but the fire investigators decided that a cigarette end was the culprit. Since both Sting and I were non-smokers, we were absolved. It was never discovered who torched The Squeaks but whoever it was deserved a medal. If Sting had not been with me on the night of the fire, I would have had deep suspicions. When hauled from the pit after our kidnapping, he had commented, 'Those fucking Squeaks are dead. I'll fucking swing for them.' It didn't help allay suspicions when Sting was heard a few days later singing 'Fire' by The Crazy World of Arthur Brown.

Soon it was time for us to leave the Madhouse of Logan and head back to St Cuthbert's for the final year. We parted on good terms with all our workmates but I knew that we had been there a little too long when I finally got round to asking Sting what he thought about the historic moon landing. 'A fucking load of shite' was his curt reply.

31 – BETTING FOR BEGINNERS

Tony, Joe, Hughie and myself had been educated to university standard so it was obvious that a great future lay ahead of us as... bookmakers! Hughie and Joe had dabbled in making a book at school with some success. Sting and I didn't have much interest in it. Sting has never been much of a gambler except at backgammon and, although I had never bet much, I did have the odd wager on the Derby and Grand National. I went along a couple of times with the lads to Gosforth Park for the horseracing. It soon became apparent that the men with the satchels were the only winners. 'You never see a poor bookie' is an old adage that I had firmly believed in, but it was to turn out to be a load of crap, however.

Hughie was the main instigator in favour of making a book. His dad liked a bet and Hughie had been gambling from the age of three, according to him. At the age of 15, he came to realise that there was more profit in taking bets than making them. But he needed partners to help his business flourish. Tony, who always seemed to have plenty of cash, and Joe were added to the board. Sting and I, who were almost permanently skint, were never asked to join the bookmaking racket. By the time we were sixth-formers, it was an open secret that, if you wanted a bet, Hughie and his partners were the men to see. On big race days, large sums of money were wagered – even some of the younger masters had a bet. I always thought that they were skating on very thin ice. If the news of their betting operation ever reached the head, they would have been out on their arses. But it never did.

When we left St Cuthbert's, we all went our separate ways. I attended Newcastle Polytechnic, later to be renamed the 'University of Northumbria'. Hughie went to St Mary's teacher training college in Leeds, majoring in 'Phys Ed'. Tony went into accountancy as an articled clerk with a view to becoming a chartered accountant. Joe went straight into a job with the Provincial Insurance Company, where he is now a senior claims investigator – after some 29 years' service. Sting went off to Warwick University where he enjoyed what can only be described as a brief flirtation with academia.

But Sting wasn't involved when the others cajoled me into joining them in forming a firm of bookmakers. The plan was simple. After a year or so, during which time we would be saving up every penny for the business, we would get a bookmaker's permit, then go on to racecourses all over the country to ply our lucrative trade. That was the theory. We had even decided on a trading name, 'Tom Hardy', though my own creation of 'Nat Sabbath', I thought, had a much more impressive ring to it. The others reckoned it sounded more like an undertaker's, so I was voted down. In fact, we never traded as Tom Hardy, since it was I who got the permit, so we simply traded under the name Jim Berryman.

I had studied Cost and Works Accountancy at the 'Poly', which turned out to be a big mistake. Before the course, I had no idea what a Cost and Works Accountant did. After a year on the course, I was still none the wiser. A combination of poor lecturers and, more importantly, a total lack of interest in the subject proved a recipe for failure. Worse still was the fact that on the same course there was a St Cuthbert's old boy, Roy Thompson. Roy had only been a fringe pal at school but now we were inseparable. Roy and I appeared to be majoring in Social Drinking. We could have gone on to first-class honours degrees in that subject, but amazingly after our first-year exam results we were thrown out. At least, I was. Roy may have left voluntarily; it's hard to say.

The rest of the lads fared a little better – none of them lost their jobs or were asked to leave work – and even Sting became semi-respectable, training to be a junior-school teacher. As far as the bookmaking business was concerned, I made the first tangible move by getting a position with a major bookmaker, though I had never had a grounding at racecourse level. The next few years passed quickly: 1975 was soon upon us and we were ready to take on the world. Sting had been teaching at St Paul's Catholic School in Cramlington on Tyneside. You might have thought he would have had enough of Catholic schools by now, but he was doing what came naturally to him. Not very good at anything, he was teaching others not to be very good at anything as well. No doubt he was teaching his pupils how to skive, never to cut their hair and how to make a mockery of religious ceremonies.

We still met up now and then, but, as my life revolved around horseracing and gambling and Sting's around music, we began to drift apart. We would meet for a drink and I would go on about the racing, while he would spout on about some unknown musician – unknown to me, that is – called Thelonius Monk. He had only been moderately interested in music at school but now he was totally immersed in it. I had heard him play the guitar but had never rated him as a budding Duane Eddy.

Nevertheless, he did play in a band, Last Exit, which I think he had formed himself, having first played with an outfit called The Big Band which had a good reputation among local jazz followers. It was around this time that Sting got his nickname, the one that most of the world knows him by today. In those days, he appeared to own only one jumper, a black-and-yellow hooped job. Someone in his band thought he looked like a bee and started calling him 'Sting'. We were having a pint together when a pal of his passed us, saying, 'Hi, Sting'. I asked him why he had called him that and he told me the jumper story. For some reason it irked me.

'You looked more like a wasp in that jumper. Why didn't he just call you "Wasp"?' I demanded.

'I suppose he thought I looked more like a bee,' he replied.

'Then why not call you "Bee", then. "Sting" sounds so pathetic,' I continued to niggle.

'Oh, I see, "Wasp" and "Bee" are all right, but "Sting" is pathetic,' he argued.

'They're all fucking pathetic, Sting! Sting, my arse!' I ranted.

'If you're so fucking bothered about the name, I'll go and get the guy and you can tell him to change it to whatever you fucking well like. OK?' he spat back.

'Listen, Gordon, it's a bloody good job you're not still wearing that crappy brown jumper you had a few weeks ago or the bloke in the band might have called you "Shite". Far more appropriate, don't you think?'

I don't know why I was so put out by the nickname bit; it may just have been that our long-lasting friendship was on the wane and this was proof that we were going in opposite directions.

We would normally have burst out laughing after a spat like that, but we sat glaring into our beer for a while before I said I was on my way. 'See you next week, "Shite"?' I ventured, not spitefully.

'Aye, next week,' 'Shite' answered with a little grin.

We parted on fairly good terms and I still went to see him perform with his band in a variety of dives around the area. One night the police raided the club where he was playing for serving 'after-hours' alcohol. We were all cautioned while Sting's band played 'The Laughing Policeman'.

I had been granted a bookmaker's betting permit and immediately applied for racecourse pitches at all the northern and some Midlands courses. Within a few weeks, the Northern Bookmakers' Protection Association informed me that I was permitted to operate as a bookmaker at several tracks in the North and Midlands. The Jim Berryman Betting Organisation was up and running. We celebrated by throwing a party. Sting came along and played a few tunes until we insisted he stopped. He was upsetting the cat.

We did have a couple of teething problems, though. Firstly, we didn't really have enough venture capital and, secondly, despite our enthusiasm none of us had ever worked at a racecourse before. Only a minor detail, we argued, since we had been going to Tony's house in Low Fell, Gateshead, every Monday night for weeks, practising taking imaginary bets which Tony, the clerk, wrote in his ledger. The phantom punters never backed a winner. I had watched the bookies at the races calling out the bets and soon picked up the knack. Tony's dad knew a real racecourse clerk, Tony Shepherdson, and he showed our Tony how to do it properly. We had one further problem. None of us had the foggiest idea about the bookmaker's most potent weapon, the 'tic-tac'.

No one we knew could tell us what these mystical signs and hand signals meant. We knew that they conveyed the odds of the horses and were used for hedging bets, but that was as far as we knew. Semaphore without the flags, we reckoned. Eventually Tony discovered a tattered old manual on odds and betting buried in the dark recesses of Newcastle Central Library. It explained the 'tic-tac'; Tony expertly amended it for our own private use.

We bought the rest of the equipment. The first item was a metal board with 'JIM BERRYMAN – NEWCASTLE' emblazoned on it. It had two blackboard strips on either side so you could chalk the odds on it. There was also a steel foldaway tripod, which extended to hold up the board, with a metal cash-tray affixed in the middle. The stuff we needed was very expensive when bought brand-new, so much so that we balked at the price of a new satchel which retailed at over £40. We eventually managed to get one gratis from an ancient bookie who had made a book at the dogs before the war – the Boer War, Tony said. It was old and small, but what could we expect for nowt?

Now we were all set, though we still had no transport. None of us owned a car and only Tony could drive anyway, but we splashed out on a Ford Escort, which tore a further big hole in our capital. We had estimated that we would need at least £400 in readies for our first day as bookies – a totally inadequate sum, in fact, but at the time ignorance was bliss. We thought that, because we would only be taking bets in the 'cheap' and 'Silver Ring' enclosures, we wouldn't need that much money to start with. We were greenhorns who would only learn through experience that our notions were entirely false.

With only a few days to go before our debut at Leicester Races, we were £100 light in our float, admittedly not a huge sum but we could not find anyone who fancied lending us this piffling amount.

It looked like the time had come for us to approach the bank. Tony arranged an appointment to see his bank manager about a business loan for the Jim Berryman Partnership. All four of the partners were asking for loans of £500. We had a carefully made-up business plan and we were smartly dressed in our best suits. As he listened to our proposals, the manager smiled broadly, then said that, if Tony put up the deeds of his house as collateral, we could have the loan. If he didn't, then we could fuck off.

Tony was as confident as the next man that we would be a success – as long as the next man wasn't this twat bank manager – but he had a natural aversion to spending life under canvas or in the care of the Salvation Army. In short, Tony wasn't prepared to put the deeds up. The bank manager was not only a belt-

and-braces man, but he also had a Velcro waistband to boot. We may have marched in, but we limped out still £100 short of our minimum stake money.

32 – STING THE BOOKIE

I thought of a potential, if unlikely, investor... Sting. I had gone to see him play at some pathetic gig and afterwards he told me that he needed money for a new guitar and had been refused a bank loan. I thought he was hinting at a loan from me, so I sat there completely comatose. If our betting partnership had been refused when we had a perfectly good business plan, what chance did 'Bert Weedon' here have? Not only should he have been refused a loan but he should also have been fined £50 for having the temerity to ask, I reckoned.

'I've saved up £100,' he bleated, 'but I need another £100.' The chances of Sting paying anyone back £100 from his trade as a musician were as remote as him being awarded the Nobel Prize for Chemistry. We sat staring each other out. Finally I cracked.

'I think I can help you get that £100, but there is just a

tiny risk involved,' I informed him. Sting was never a gambler at heart, so I wasn't that confident he would bite.

'What sort of risk are we talking about. It isn't the kind where I stand to lose my liberty by any chance, is it?' Sting enquired.

Tammy Wynette's 'Stand By Your Man' blasted out from the jukebox. Sting sang along for a few bars to the chagrin of everyone within earshot.

'The tiny risk is that you can make £100 no bother, but you will have to risk your £100 to get it,' I explained.

'Are you taking the piss?' he replied.

'You know that the lads and me are going to Leicester Races this Saturday to make a book,' I said, dangling the bait.

'I think you may have mentioned it a few dozen times,' he answered. Sarcasm was starting to become his strong point.

'I will be able to cut you in if I have a word with the partners,' I promised.

'Cut me in? You mean put money up for you to bet with at the races? Are you fucking kidding, have you any idea how long I have to work to make £100? And you want me to give it to you to blow at the fucking races, this is a wind-up, right?'

'If you were waiting to make £100 from one of these gigs, you could wait fifty years. How much did you get paid tonight? Three quid, scampi and chips, and two bottles of Mackeson, wasn't it?'

He grimaced. I was right.

'So you really think I could win £100 in one day at the races?' he said, softening.

'Of course you can. If you gave us £100 for your ante and we put up £300, then you would have a quarter share in the profit for the day. If we won, say, £400, you would make £100 pure profit, simple!' I told him.

'That seems fair enough, but what makes you think you are bound to win and what's my fucking "auntie" got to do with it?' Sting asked, confused.

'Not your auntie, you thick twat, your "A-N-T-E", you know, stake money! And don't fucking dare ask about a sirloin or a T-bone,' I added before he got too smart for his own good. 'You must know that bookies don't lose. It will be a piece of piss,' I argued as he pulled faces at me.

'Obviously I know that. What I can't figure out is this: if you can't lose, why do you want my money?' he muttered. The bastard wasn't as thick as I thought.

'Because I'm your pal. You don't think I've been walking the streets, looking for people who want a piece of the action, do you?' I coaxed, despite the fact that was almost exactly what I had been doing.

'So you just want to do me a favour?' he said in mock innocence.

'Sure. The chance of you losing your stake money is negligible.'

'Oh, go on then. You can have my £100 and I look forward to getting £200 back if it's as easy as you say,' he finally agreed.

'Good lad! You know it makes sense,' I congratulated

him on being conned. 'You could win even more than your £100 if things go well; Tony reckons we will win a monkey at least,' I informed the new bookie.

His face changed. 'What in fuck's name would you want with a monkey?' he demanded.

He must have thought that this was the racecourse equivalent of winning a goldfish at the fair.

'A "monkey", you dozy get, is slang for £500,' I told him to his relief. His reluctance to own a monkey made sense. I had a relative who had one as a pet and its party trick was to piss in the teapot. It also tried to shag my dad. I didn't want to go through that again.

Sting pulled out a wad of one-pound notes from his tattered jeans. Just as I was about to wrestle them from his grasp, he suddenly pulled back, asking coyly, 'How will I know how much we have won? There could be a miscalculation, you know, a mistake or something...'

I rounded on him. 'Oh, here we go... I haven't seen the colour of your money yet and already you fear a conspiracy to cheat you out of your winnings! Would I rob you? Would any of the lads? We're not just some gits, like your band members who you have only known for five minutes. If you think we're going to have you over, don't fucking bother giving me your cash. I try to do you a favour and...'

'All right, all right, don't blow a fuse. I believe you,' he concluded.

The bullshit had worked. He handed me his grubby smeck of folding stuff.

'I'm not doing anything on Saturday anyway, so I think I might go to the races with you,' Sting announced much to my consternation.

It wasn't that we were going to cheat him, just that there was a far greater chance of us losing his guitar money than I had admitted. If he wanted to go, though, I would not stand in his way.

Only a couple of days before we were due to make our debuts, Joe Bulman phoned to say that he would not be able to make it. It was his dad's greyhound's *bar mitzvah* or something. Joe was the 'tic-tac' man and therefore possibly the most important member of the team. We needed a replacement at very short notice. Insanely, we thought of Sting. I told him that he was now required to be an integral part of the team and he must learn 'tic-tac' from the book – he had two days in which to master it!

He argued vehemently that he would be useless and he could never learn the skill in two days, but now we had his cash he was in no position to say no. He spent the next two days dutifully stuck in the house going over and over all the tic-tac signs until he had a working knowledge of the art. Why we thought he could do it, God alone knows. A meerkat would have had a better chance of learning Calculus.

33 – TO LEICESTER AND PENZANCE

Saturday was upon us and, after a sleepless night, the intrepid bunch set off for Leicester. Me, Tony, Hughie and a nervous member of a beat combo commenced our first foray into the hostile world of racecourse bookmaking. As we began our long drive south, only Hughie was confident of a lucrative start. By the time we got there, he had talked us all round. We arrived at Leicester Races on a lovely spring day in April 1975 and quickly got all of our gear from the car, making sure Sting humped most of it so he'd look like a real worker. Although the partners were smartly dressed, Sting looked like he had spent the night in a wind tunnel.

We paid to enter the Silver Ring of the course, then I went to buy the betting badge which was necessary if we wanted to stand up and take bets at the track. A miserable-looking official looked down the list of approved bookmakers to see my name right at the bottom of the list.

'New boy?' he asked with all the charisma of a Nazi storm trooper.

'Yeah, first day today. I hope a few outsiders go in,' I tried by way of conversation.

'Sign here,' he said, ignoring me.

The four of us walked into the betting ring and headed for the back row to set up for business. We thought it only right that Sting should put up our joint, the betting stand, as we had better things to do – like having a beer and a sandwich. Half an hour later he joined us in the bar.

'Thanks very much, bastards. That was worse than the fucking *Krypton Factor*.'

'It's all good experience for you,' I argued, knowing that this would be his first and last trip with us.

'All the bookies were laughing at me but I put it up eventually. Has nobody got me a beer?' he moaned. We told him to shut up and listen.

'You are confident that you know the tic-tac, Sting?' we asked.

'It was easier than I thought. I just copied it from the book,' he replied with confidence.

'Right, let's get out there and cane those punters' arses,' Hughie asserted, taking charge.

We strode purposefully from the bar, sending Sting into the Tattersalls betting ring, the main betting area. He was supposed to get himself three wooden boxes and stand on them so we could see him above the crowd. Then he would convey the odds of each horse in the first race by means of tic-tac, the hand and arm movements that we, and hopefully he, knew by heart.

The rest of us went over to our joint. I could feel the malevolent eyes of the other bookies burning into the back of my neck. I heard an anonymous voice shout out, 'Look at this bunch of wallies; they're as green as grass. I hope they've brought their piggy banks with them!' I was mortified. I thought that the older bookies might have taken us under their wings and shown us the ropes. In the event, they just stood glaring at us, taking the piss. I looked at our betting bag and realised that it was tiny in comparison with the other bookies' satchels.

One of the bookies must have read my mind. He called out, 'Holy Jesus! Look at their itsy-bitsy hod. You won't get a ten-bob note in there! It's his mum's purse, he's brought his mum's purse!' he chanted. A wizened old layer was shouting at the top of his voice, pointing at us. I felt like I was back at school and, now that the pupils were being put in streams according to penis size in front of the entire assembly, I was informed I had been demoted to 5D.

Hughie reacted angrily. 'If you all think it is so funny, why don't you come and laugh in my face?' he shouted to the ring. Hughie may have been a rookie in the business but he looked like he could punch your lights out. The laughing stopped, with nervous coughs taking over. I thought that, if we had called the firm 'Nat Sabbath', no one would have dared take the mickey.

It was time to take bets. The card began with a horrible race: a 'Ladies' race with 25 runners, a tic-tac's nightmare. Since most of the bookmakers were chalking up the odds, it was time for us to do likewise. Sting was up on his boxes and he waved to us to indicate that he was ready to 'tic-tac' the prices to us. He started slowly and deliberately. It was complete gibberish. It looked at first hand as if he was doing it right, but although familiar the signs he gave out meant nothing to anyone.

'What the fucking hell is that idiot playing at?' Hughie shouted after watching him give a so-called 'betting show'.

I looked over to see Sting waving away with gay abandon. Hughie was right. He was making up his own signs. My eyes bulged in their sockets.

'Ignore that nutter,' I called out. 'Get the odds from the bookies around us.'

Business was slow but we took a few bets, the odds copied from the nearby bookmakers. Interest in the race seemed to centre on a nag called Boy Desmond. Suddenly there was a run on the horse as it was backed at all rates from 4/1 to 6/4. Before we knew where we were, Boy Desmond – despite my lowering its price – was a massive loser in our book. Tony eventually got round to calculating the risk we faced; if the horse won, it would lose us £390. That would mean we would only have what was in our pockets to get us home – this was turning into a nightmare.

Despite the fact we were completely ignoring him, Sting was still doing his stuff. Hughie had motioned for him to desist from his random ravings but he kept up his pretence that he was a tic-tac man.

When I told Hughie that Boy Desmond could single-handedly bankrupt us, he went berserk. He argued that we should hedge our bets but time was running out. He rushed around the ring trying to back the horse at almost any price to reduce our liabilities but all the books were in the same boat. No one wanted to lay the horse. We were stuck. The race was off and Boy Desmond, if he won, would wipe us out.

Sting arrived on the scene. 'Did I do all right, lads?' he asked to groans all round.

'FUCK OFF!' we shouted in unison.

Hughie's face was purple. His realisation that this could be the quickest demise in bookmaking history was taking its toll.

'We'll have to fuck off after one bastard race! Can you imagine the shame? These bookies will never stop laughing!'

Sting looked bemused. 'You don't mean we might lose on this race, do you, Hughie?' he asked with great understatement.

The race was nearing its conclusion as we stood there in a funereal huddle, hoping against hope that Boy Desmond would not prevail. The field flashed past us, the course commentator's voice drowned out by the roars of the crowd. 'Photograph,' he called. We hadn't lost just yet. It was a photo-finish between the damned Boy Desmond and an outsider, Penzance, but things looked bad. It appeared to all and sundry that the favourite had just held on for a win. We were desolate as we awaited the official result.

'I'm afraid we're fucked, gentlemen, sorry,' I announced as it was probably my fault the horse had lost us so much money, though tic-tac man Sting had been a major contributor, too.

Sting and Hughie were quietly arguing the toss before Hughie calmly informed us that the reason Sting's tic-tac was nonsense was because he had learned it by looking in the mirror. His signs were all about-face. I didn't know whether to laugh or cry. Then the course commentator made up my mind.

'First, number twenty, Penzance, the winner,' he announced to boundless joy within the Jim Berryman Organisation. As the three of us danced a jig, Sting stood looking perplexed. The result might just as well have been Rudolph the Red-Nosed Reindeer by a nose for all that Sting knew about the situation. 'We won, I take it,' Sting said before he ambled off, presumably to find the stall where he could win a monkey.

The rest of the day, we used him to go and get the teas or place the odd bet. With no more Boy Desmonds lurking, we survived the remainder of the meeting and, when the last race was over, we calculated that, after expenses, we had won almost exactly £400. Sting had won his guitar money, after all.

34 – THE LAW OF DIMINISHING RETURNS

Leaving the track, we had waved a cheery goodbye to the miserable bookies at Leicester and heard an unintelligible grunt in return, but we were euphoric.

We had taken them on as well as the punters and, despite the vain 'Mirror-man' Sting's efforts to send us into premature liquidation, we had won handsomely.

On the way home, John Lennon's version of 'Stand By Me' was playing on the car radio and, as was his wont, Sting joined in. When he had finished injuring the song, Sting smiled and winked at me. He said that he could acquire a taste for the racing game, conveniently forgetting his back-to-front tic-tac antics and the first-race fiasco. I told him that, if he learned the tic-tac properly this time, there was no reason why he shouldn't come racing with us again. Not many miles up the road, we decided to stop for fish and chips at a takeaway.

Tony and I wanted fish and chips, Hughie pie and chips but Sting had his eye on something that we hadn't experienced in the North-East before – a doner kebab. The foreign owner asked, 'Weesh one you wan' feesh?'

Tony and I nodded.

'Weesh one you wan' pie?'

Hughie indicated that was him.

'And weesh one you wan' kebab?'

Sting was still counting his money and was oblivious to the man's question.

'Weesh one you wan' kebab?' he repeated.

'What did he say?' Sting asked of Tony.

'I think he wants to know which one of us is "Wanky Bob"?' he replied. 'I can only assume he means you, Gordon.'

'You wan' kebab?' the man asked Sting.

'Yes, I'm "Wanky Bob", that's me,' Sting replied, suppressing a giggle as he was handed his supper.

He told Tony that only his mam called him Gordon now, for which he received a barbed reply. 'For Christ's sake, how many fucking aliases have you got? First it was "Gordon", then "Noddy", then "Sting" and now it's fucking "Wanky Bob". I should stick to Sting if I were you, Wanky.'

Sting only smiled weakly before laying into his kebab. Back on the road, Sting solemnly informed us that he was hoping to go to London soon to try and make it big in the pop world. We wished him luck. He said he had bandied about a few names for a new group.

'What's wrong with "Wanky Bob and the Tossers"?' Tony argued, whereas Hughie's best effort was 'Kendal Morecambe and the Lakes'. When Sting settled for the rather more banal 'The Police', we were gutted.

But our talk of making thousands at bookmaking was starting to rub off on Sting. 'You lucky lads now have £200 of my dosh,' he announced, 'and I expect you will give it to me before we part.' We grunted our reluctant assent. 'Supposing that I let you keep hold of it for now, and you used it as part of your float for the next race meeting. If you put in, say, £600 and me £200, I would take a quarter of the profit just like today. You would have a bigger float and be able to lay bigger bets, so win more money.' This lad was learning fast. Clueless that morning, by evening he was wheeler-dealing his way to a small fortune by sound investment. We had been grateful for his money that day, but we did not need another partner, just a mug with a few quid to spare.

'Look, Gordon,' Tony niggled, reading the other partners' thoughts, 'if we keep going like this, you will have a bigger share of the business than we will; you will end up being the bookie and we will have to form a fucking band!'

'Nat Sabbath and the Welshers,' Sting countered. 'Look, I don't want to be a partner any more than you want me to be one. I just thought an extra few quid for your first couple of meetings would come in handy, that's all. You all know that I haven't got the foggiest idea about bookmaking. It's just a short-term arrangement.'

'Very well, young man, we will keep your guitar money for the time being and will probably turn it into a six-piece ensemble, starting at Wetherby on Wednesday night,' I answered for all of us without any dissent.

'Wednesday is no good for me,' Sting said. 'I've got a gig then at the Christian Science Centre in Dunston.'

'The frigging where? No, I remember now. I went to one of the services once, devoted to Our Lady of Sulphuric Acid,' I teased.

'It was nitric acid actually, Jim,' Sting retorted. 'I can't miss the gig.'

'There's nothing to stop your money from coming to Wetherby, is there?' I asked.

Sting hummed and hawed, before agreeing that his cash could accompany us to Wetherby.

We went to Wetherby with his money, and that was the last he ever saw of it. We did it all in – and all ours too for that matter. A string of successful favourites reduced us to paupers. And we in turn had reduced Sting to a man who could not afford a comb and paper, let alone a brand-new guitar.

I telephoned him late that night with the bad news. I told him exactly what had happened, informing him that he could inspect the field book which recorded the bets struck. He told me that, at the concert, he had experienced a terrible feeling of foreboding and, in a way, had been expecting this call. I had been waiting for a torrent of abuse, or even tears, at the demise of his cash, but his philosophical acceptance of the news was impressive. I thanked him for his compassion and understanding.

'It's not your fault, Jim,' Sting said quietly. 'I should never have become involved with a two-bit, pissant, bunch of clueless, brainless wankers,' he said, showing not only compassion but also great perception.

'Never mention bookmaking to me again or talk to me about your moronic partners, where racing is concerned. Do that and we will remain friends,' he concluded.

Somehow Sting was soon to become a famous pop personality and I think he has probably forgiven us by now. He never did get the new guitar. He kept his old one for a few years more and he always looked upon it as his lucky charm, so perhaps the loss of his money was a blessing in disguise, a bloody good disguise though.

Doing his money at the races obviously spurred Sting on to success as a pop star. In fact, it could be argued that it would never have happened for the boy without my help. Has he ever thanked me? Has he buggery! There's just no pleasing some people.

35 – ON THE WAY TO BEVERLEY ILLS

S ting was as good as his word and played no further part in our bookmaking business. And, after being cleaned out at only our second meeting, we needed to do some serious borrowing. The bank, we thought, was slightly less likely to lend us the money now, considering our business had lasted only two working days. It appeared that the bank manager's pessimism had been well founded. In the event, Tony's dad came to the rescue, loaning the firm enough cash to get us back on an even keel and back on the racecourse.

Meanwhile, Sting had begun work as a primary school teacher in Cramlington, Northumberland; at nights he continued to play in the kind of clubs and pubs which no one in their right mind would go drinking in. The lads would attend some of these gigs, sometimes as bodyguards since the crowd could turn ugly because

Sting was in the habit of insulting his audience if he did not get their strict attention when he was playing. 'I reckon the IQ in this room is nearly 120,' he suddenly said one night. 'Not on average, though, that's the whole fucking lot of you added together!' Not long afterwards, he avoided a flying stool with great expertise.

Sting decided that his talents were wasted in the North-East and that he was going to seek his fortune in the capital. By then he had married Frances and was a father to boot with a young son called Joe... and he still had the cheek to call me a gambler. I wondered about his sanity and he about mine as I continued to try and make a living as a bookie. Despite all our misgivings, he went to London and, as always, we wished him every success and told him that, when he returned, there was always the offer of a job as a tic-tac – for his wife anyway. When he got to London, he signed on the dole and spent a lot of time on the floor of a friend's flat in Kensington, writing daft songs and sleeping there, too.

A few months after his departure, I was watching television at home and, while channel surfing, I came across *Rock Goes to College* on BBC2. I knew that Sting had formed a new band, The Police, with Stewart Copeland and Andy Summers and, lo and behold, there they were on TV with Sting fronting the band and belting out 'Roxanne' to a college audience. Sting had always hated students and now here he was pandering to their pathetic whims. I immediately phoned all the lads, telling them to tune in and watch our tic-tac man making an arse of himself.

He scowled and strutted around the stage as if I had just phoned him with the news of his cash disappearing at Wetherby. I had no idea why he looked so angry; perhaps it was something to do with his hairdresser since he now sported a bizarre shock of blond hair. His natural colour is a rich hue of mouse.

Since Sting's move to London, only Hughie had kept in touch with him via copious letters but soon all we got from Sting was that sourpuss look through our TV sets, newspapers and magazines as his group received more and more media exposure. The Police's first single, 'Fall Out', was only popular with people who wore tattered rags for clothes and its lyrics consisted of two words, one of which was 'off'.

Their second record was 'Roxanne', which was about a prostitute, ensuring that it would not get played on Radio 1 despite good reviews. If Sting wrote this song from personal experience, I can assure you that it did not occur on his native Tyneside. We do not go in for that sort of thing up here. That's because we are too preoccupied with football, gambling, whippets, leeks and boozing. Recreational sex is unheard of... we leave that to soft Southerners.

A few months later when Sting and his band were quite well known and Sting could almost be called 'famous', I was walking down Northumberland Street in Newcastle, when I heard a familiar voice boom out, 'Yo! Berryman'.

I turned to see Sting waving at me from across the road. I went to shake hands with him only for him to embrace me warmly.

'It's great to see you, man. How's it going? Made your fortune yet?' Sting greeted me.

'Never mind me, what about you, you jammy bastard? You're never off the telly!' I answered.

'Yeah, it's fantastic, isn't it? Things are getting more exciting by the second,' Sting said.

'What are you doing among us plebs? Are you not too famous to be walking around town without a paper bag on your head?' I asked.

'Well, a few people have asked me for an autograph and I've noticed people pointing at me and nudging each other and so on. I'll just have to get used to it, I suppose.'

'Why are you here, though, answering bail?' I joked.

'I've just come home for a few days to see my folks. They've not been well.'

'I'm sorry to hear that, kidda. How's the family?'

'Champion, I've left them back home. For the first time in ages, I've got some time to myself, but I still miss them.'

'This is a bit of a long shot, but me and the boys are going to Beverley Races tomorrow. You're quite welcome to come along if you fancy it. It's a two-day meeting, so we'll be staying overnight.'

'Do I buggery fancy it! You do remember the last time I went racing with you?'

'It wasn't that bad,' I insisted.

'It fucking well was! You lost all my money!' he countered.

'No, we didn't. We won money at Leicester. It was at Wetherby where we did your cobblers in.'

'It doesn't matter where it was. All I know was that I was potless for weeks.'

'Ah, come on, let's not haggle over ancient history. You might never get the chance for some fun with the lads for years to come,' I said prophetically.

'Well, I don't know,' he mused, rubbing his chin.

'I don't suppose that you are now so famous that the race-goers of Beverley are going to tear your clothes off,' I argued.

'They might not tear my clothes off but I've got the distinct impression I may end up losing my shirt!' Sting said with sarcasm.

'Look, the firm is no longer operating on a shoestring. We won't be asking you to contribute any of your considerable wealth. Come on, man, two days at the races in July at Beverley, lovely place. Drink a few beers, make a few quid, have some laughs.'

We chewed the fat for a bit longer over a pint in the Northumberland Arms, before I persuaded the rock star that the trip would be good fun. I told him that he must not wear any pop-star clothing to bring attention to himself, although I thought the chance of Sting's fame reaching the far-flung post of Humberside was remote.

'I don't wear my stage clothes all the time, you

know. Do I look like Liberace now, for instance?' he argued back.

'No, you look like a bucket of shit,' I said.

'Fair comment,' he agreed.

'Will we be staying in an hotel?' Sting asked.

'Something like that,' I lied. 'See you tomorrow, ten o'clock in the Haymarket. Don't be late, or we'll go without you,' I added.

'Fuck off,' he answered.

What I had not told Sting was that we were cutting down on expenses and we would not be staying in what he laughably referred to as 'an hotel'. Hughie had borrowed a massive tent from the school where he taught and that would be our accommodation for the night. It was mid-summer; it would not be that bad, would it?

But if Sting thought he was going to make it to Beverly Hills, he was going to get there via the hills of Beverley.

36 – HE DROVE IT RIGHT ON TO THE GREEN

We all met up at ten o'clock the following day in Newcastle's Haymarket. Sting had dressed casually. 'Hedge' and 'backwards' were the words that first sprang to mind. We were soon on our way to Beverley Races after Sting had greeted those who had not seen him in the last twelve months. Though Sting did not know it yet, Hughie had told us that he had brought everything that was essential for the camping aspect of our trip. What he should have said was that he had brought everything essential for him and fuck the rest of us.

We got to the races and it was a lovely evening, so we hoped to do a roaring trade even if we were in the course enclosure in the middle of the track where the punters were much more likely to be picnickers than hardened gamblers.

We started the betting, as Sting went walk-about with no one taking a blind bit of notice of the rock star among their number. For us, it was hard going. The tight-fisted punters of Beverley could count change without taking their hands out of their pockets. If anyone else asked me for a 'dollar' (25p) on a horse, I would have screamed. The field book was black with figures but after the first race we had taken little more than £100. That was repeated throughout the evening but at the end of the meeting we had won £200, mostly in coins by the look of it.

Sting had mooched around looking inconspicuous and having the odd bet, though not with us. 'I would never have been paid any winnings,' he correctly argued.

'Right, how about a drink back at the hotel?' Sting asked.

'Hotel!' said Hughie. 'What fucking hotel? We're all sleeping in a tent. Didn't anybody tell you, Sting?'

'No, they fucking well didn't,' he answered, looking me squarely in the eye.

Sting had not camped out since he was 11 years old. He was not the only one.

'I'm not sleeping in a bastard tent! I'm used to comfort. I've got my reputation to uphold, you know,' Sting raved.

'And we've got a tent to uphold,' Tony answered laconically.

'You've got two options, Sting. You can go and find a nice hotel in town or you can sleep with the rest of the low-lifes. It's up to you,' I told him.

'Look, I'll pay for the lot of us, but I'm buggered if I'm spending a night under the stars,' Sting insisted. He phoned every hotel and guest house in Beverley and got the same response: there was no room at the inn. 'It's the races, you know.'

Sting finally succumbed to his fate. He decided that a surfeit of alcohol was the only answer and downed as many beers as he could in the time available. 'Right, lads,' I shouted. 'A night under the stars with only three twats for company.'

Tony, the only one of us who was sober, drove us away into the darkness, searching for a farmer's field to pitch our tent for the night. He finally drove off the road on to some likely-looking ground. He stopped the engine.

'This looks like a nice flat bit, men. We'll put the tent up here,' Tony said, the only sane one among us.

Hughie, who could barely stand through overindulgence, decided to take charge. Hughie's insistence that the tent was a bell-tent was not borne out either by the shape of the canvas or the number of guy-ropes and tent-pegs, but it was erected as though it were a bell-tent and, as a result, there was a big gap between the bottom of the tent and the ground. Sixteen guy-ropes had been hammered into the turf to secure the structure, which now looked like it was hovering in the air, a foot above the ground. We were now exhausted, so bell-tent or not it would have to do.

'If this is a bell-tent, I'm a fucking werewolf,' Sting

observed, surveying the monstrosity. 'I'm fucked if I'm sleeping in that thing. I'll doss down in the car.'

'So will I,' Tony quickly followed.

'I guess that just leaves us two pioneers, eh, Hubert, my scout-minded pal. And may I say, pissed as I am, I have never in all my bastard life been involved in a bigger farce than putting up this frigging tent.' I slunk off into the darkness.

I turned to view my audience but they had gone off. Sting and Tony disappeared into the relative comfort of the car, leaving Hughie and me in isolation. I fumbled my way into the tent where Hughie was already ensconced. I asked him for my sleeping bag.

'What sleeping bag?' he slurred.

'I take it that you are joking. The sleeping bag that you said you would be bringing, oh expedition leader,' I reminded him.

'I've only got one. Obviously I thought you would bring your own, didn't I?' he replied.

'But you said you would bring everything for us, you useless shite. Can't I get in with you? It looks big enough,' I implored.

'Fuck off is it!' he said sympathetically.

I decided to try the car, approaching with great stealth before peering inside. 'Come on, lads, let me in. Hughie's burned the tent down trying to light his farts!'

I received a muffled reply of rasps, moans, burps and belches. I tried the doors. The bastards had locked themselves in. The boot was open and I noticed my full-length leather coat. If it got cold I might need that, I reckoned.

I re-entered the tent to find McBride comatose. He had been so concerned that I might freeze to death, he had immediately fallen asleep. At least he had managed to seal up the gap at the bottom of the tent by stuffing old copies of the *Sporting Life* into it. Remarkably, I nodded straight off only to wake up very cold in the wee small hours. I tried putting my leather coat on, but my feet and legs were still frozen, so I decided to take off my trousers and put my legs into the sleeves of my coat. That seemed to be much warmer and I dropped off again.

When I next regained consciousness, it was getting light again. Hughie had gone, abducted by gypsies I hoped. I was dreadfully hungover and I could hear familiar voices from outside: 'Holy Jesus!', 'Christ all fucking mighty!' and many similar profanities.

'Come on, Berryman! We're out of here!' I heard Sting shout.

I got to my feet and then fell flat on my face when I tried to take a step. During my sleep I had pushed my legs right through the armholes of my coat and I was stuck fast. I could only bunny-hop out of the tent, holding the coat-tails up to my chest. I looked like a demented kangaroo. I bounded into view but no one paid me any heed. It was no wonder that the ground we had pitched the tent on was flat. We had erected it on the sixth green of Beverley Golf Course! Even the flag had been used to help keep the tent up!

The green now had innumerable gouge marks hacked into its previously manicured surface. We tore the tent down in seconds, although in my leather-bound condition, I wasn't much use.

'You're not stuck in that coat, are you, by any chance?' Sting finally asked.

'Why, whatever gave you that idea?' I replied.

'If that's your attitude, you can just hop it!' he howled, as we scampered back into the car.

We sped off into town to get away from the scene of the crime and also to get a full English breakfast down our necks, not to mention having me extricated from the confines of my coat. Sting said I looked like a tall wallet. I hopped around the cafe to yelps of derision from friends and strangers alike and I had to wait in the stifling leather until the hardware shop opened and they cut me free, at which point they stopped laughing.

At the races that afternoon, we again won a couple of hundred quid and I vowed never to go camping again. Overnight stays would be in proper digs from then on and I still wince when I look at any green on a golf course, even if our destruction of that turf had been accidental and, in a way, celebrity sabotage is not so frowned upon, I hope. Back in Newcastle we dropped Sting off, exchanged insults and said our fond farewells. Little did I know then, but this would be a long goodbye. It was to be eight years before we would meet again.

37 – A STORMY REUNION

The next eight years of Sting's life have been well documented and, in all truth, I am not in a position to embellish the account. Firstly with The Police and then as a solo artist, he became a megastar of the pop world, with hit singles, best-selling albums and sold-out world tours. He even delved into the world of celluloid with what can only be described as mixed success. In all this time, we never spoke once. He returned to Tyneside occasionally to see his family and both his parents died prematurely, which was a great loss to him. He particularly adored his mam, Audrey.

He also appeared in concert several times in the area but I never attended, though Hughie and some old pals went and said that he had asked after me.

These years were not too kind to me and I slid down the slippery slope to insolvency. The on-course firm eventually folded. Hughie still teaches but holds a betting permit and has a sideline in betting at northern racetracks. Tony is a company director in Northumberland and Joe is still with Provincial Insurance. Meanwhile Sting is an international superstar and I became a government statistic.

Sting was someone who I used to know and love like a brother, but by 1986 I could no longer call him my friend. If I had not seen or even spoken to him during all this time, it seemed like a reasonable assumption. Surely we no longer had anything in common, apart from our schoolday memories. His public persona of smug superstar making po-faced pronouncements on issues such as the rainforests and drug-taking endeared him to very few observers, me included. If he were like that all the time, I wasn't missing much. The Gordon Sumner I had known would have said of the rainforests, 'Went there, pissed down all day, came home,' but now he had apparently changed beyond recognition.

Things were taken out of my hands by a chance meeting. Mick Millar, who had also been a pupil at St Cuthbert's but was a year younger than me, lived nearby and had been a good friend for many years. Mick is a genuine brain-box, but like me a bit of a waster. He would rather lie in bed than mow the lawn any day of the week. His weakness for a bet and undying devotion to Newcastle United cemented our friendship. Mick lives on his own, has the most complicated love life I have ever come across and has spent so much time on the dole he once went to their departmental Christmas party. He's had a job on the oil rigs for the last few years – as an administrator not a roustabout, as he proudly informs lady friends – which has confounded his critics. Still with a full head of hair, painfully thin and with a ridiculously large member, he invades my air space on a regular basis. He also became a go-between for Sting and me to get back in touch.

Mick had seen an advert in the local press, seeking extras for *Stormy Monday*, a film that was being made on Tyneside and which starred, among others, my old pal Sting. Without telling me, Mick went along to try and get in a crowd scene, which might not have paid much but it was still a day out – sad bastard!

What followed was conveyed to me by Millar, so its veracity must be taken on trust. Mick said he was standing among the other potential extras – people with one ear, no legs, dressed in army fatigues etc – when Sting spotted the smartly dressed Millar amid the sorry mob. Sting is then supposed to have elbowed his way through the crowds of unwashed, picking Millar out because he recognised him as a St Cuthbert's 'old boy'.

'Hello, Mick,' Sting is reported to have said. 'How are you doing, still living in Forest Hall, mixed-up sex life, on the dole, supporting the Toon, refusing to mow your lawn? I thought so! Come with me. I'll sort you out.'

Whatever the truth was, Mick ended up with the part of 'The Lawyer' in the film, despite cries from the other extras who were surely shouting, 'Take me, Sting, not that skinny lecherous twat!'

Mick told Sting of his friendship with me and he answered by asking Mick to bring me along one night to the set of *Stormy Monday*. When Mick told me of Sting's request, I had mixed feelings. I quite fancied seeing him again but hoped that I would not be out of my depth. After all, with his worldwide celebrity and wealth, how could I, a skint Geordie waster, have anything to talk to him about? I supposed that I would find that out.

Because of pouring rain, filming was abandoned for the night, so Mick told me that Sting would meet us in the pub nearest to the set, the Newcastle Arms, as it was then called. We sat in the pub waiting for the star. The door swung open and in walked a confident, manly figure, a man who knew precisely who he was. Sting walked in right behind him. I rose to meet my old friend, who reached out to grab me in true showbiz style, saying, 'Jim, you old rogue! You haven't changed a bit!' and giving a violent bear hug to a stranger sitting next to me. I tapped Sting on the shoulder. He turned around, dropping the impostor like a hot brick as soon as he saw me, and repeated his greeting. He quickly snapped out of showbiz celeb mode, exclaiming, 'Fucking hell, you're fat!'

The formalities over, Sting sat down in my seat and waited for me to get him a drink. Some things never change. I bought him a pint of lager without asking him what he wanted. I fancied that he might have acquired expensive tastes of late. He slurped the lager down with the minimum of fuss. We talked about this and that for a bit, nothing too heavy, and, although he had started by talking in an accent-less kind of mid-Atlantic drawl, he quickly dropped into the local vernacular without prompting. Perhaps he was an actor, after all.

Notwithstanding Sting's natural reluctance to go to the bar, the night went well. We caught up with the gossip more or less on equal terms despite his life having been slightly more interesting than mine just recently.

We were joined for a while by one of Sting's co-stars in the film, the American film star Melanie Griffith, though in all honesty I had never heard of her at the time. Sting told me she was married to Don Johnson but as I thought he was the manager of Darlington Football Club I wasn't too impressed. She had a little squeaky voice and could not understand a word I said, so it was not exactly a partnership made in heaven. She did have terrific legs, though – almost as good as her mum's, the veteran film star Tippi Hedren, who also showed up for a while and looked the epitome of a Hollywood star. Melanie listened politely while Sting translated what I was saying before shoving off to find someone who could speak English, a bit of a problem in a pub on Newcastle's fashionable Quayside.

Quite a few of the pub's customers asked Sting for his autograph. He was signing them willy-nilly, until I told him that he should sign his own name. On one occasion after getting Sting's autograph, a girl hopefully asked me, 'Are you anybody?' To which Sting answered, 'Yes, of course he is. He's Fat-Berryman-san, the Geordie Sumo wrestler.' She gave us both a quizzical look as I snatched her bit of paper and added my autograph to her collection.

The night ended on a convivial note with Sting swearing that he would keep in touch. He borrowed his taxi fare back to his hotel, leaving Mick and me standing in the pouring rain with only our bus fares home. On our way back home, I told Mick that I still liked Sting a lot and I didn't think that he was anything like the self-important tosser who often leered out of my TV screen. I had really enjoyed our night out but I was far from sure that Sting's stated commitment to cement our old friendship would bear any fruit. I hoped it would though.

Stormy Monday was a critical success, which surprised me because I thought it was a load of shite. A paper-thin plot sees Sean Bean-Seen Bean-Shawn Born (you can't have it all ways) go from toilet cleaner to hitman within 24 hours. Melanie Griffith trundles around looking sexy but bored, remarkably keeping her clothes on for most of the film. Tommy Lee Jones could have played his part as the ruthless American gangster in a coma, while Sting looks like he has spent his evenings sleeping in a cardboard box under the Tyne Bridge. Some of the continuity errors are howlers, particularly Sting with a 'five o'clock shadow' on his chin one minute, clean-shaven the next... with the stubble back in place moments later.

One man saved the film... Mick Millar. Although his role could be mistaken by the ignorant as being a mere cameo since he is only on camera for a minute or so, he bestrode the silver screen like a colossus of cinema. In his scene as 'The Lawyer', where he signs legal documents in the jazz club office, he is confronted by what seems to be the entire cast crammed into a tiny space.

His face is that of a man who could have single-handedly rescued this trash from the oblivion it so richly deserves. His menacing steely-eyed glare, glowering out at the villains, terrified me. His granite countenance focused unerringly on his accusers – chin set defiantly forward, eyes piercing – is one of the great moments in cinema history. I gasped in appreciation at what Mick had achieved on his screen debut – one day an unemployable wanker, the next a giant among thespians. It was a great tragedy that it was only I who had picked up on this riveting performance. Incredibly, it was Millar's first and last film.

It nearly proved to be Sting's last film, too. Was it mere coincidence that it was several years before he appeared again in a significant role and that, when he did – taking the part of the AC/DC butler in *The Grotesque* – the film was co-produced by Sting's wife Trudie? I think not. After watching some of his other films like *Dune* and *The Bride*, I strongly advised him never to forget how to play the guitar. I told him that he should stick to what he does best, strutting moodily around a stage, howling out a depressing dirge while faced by a morose crowd of silent sycophants.

38 - ABSENT FRIENDS

Sting and Millar completed their film and I didn't see Sting again for a while. To my surprise he did phone me sometimes, often from abroad. He would put the shits up me by phoning in the middle of the night from the USA to inform me that he was bored and wanted to speak to someone who did not automatically agree with every word he said. Since I disagreed with virtually every word he said, I was a good choice even if I was a few thousand miles away. He was obviously missing Andy Summers and Stewart Copeland who had raised arguing with him to an art form, plus the fact that I was unlikely to kick him in the bollocks over the phone. His 'nads had taken a bit of a pounding in The Police when the three of them had one of their legendary battles.

Sting continued his bonding with the odd letter and call before telling me he was on tour in the UK soon and he would be performing two concerts at Newcastle City Hall. He asked if I would deign to attend and, this time, I agreed. The tour was to promote Sting's latest album, *The Soul Cages*, a sombre, introspective piece of work and a clear look back at his North-East roots. Sting once described Newcastle as 'a good place to bring up your sick', which I know was intended as a joke but which had offended some locals. Whatever has been said before, Sting is, I know, as proud of being a Geordie as any Newcastle United replica shirt-wearing boozer in the Bigg Market on a Friday night.

As I was now on speaking terms with the great man, it was entirely appropriate that I should swell the ranks of his audience. Best of all, I would be depriving him of the price of admission: I was on the guest list.

Hughie and I went along with another old school pal, Dave Bradshaw, who had become a successful solicitor in Newcastle. I had not seen Dave since leaving school, but despite a little weight gained and a little hair lost he was instantly recognisable.

By this time, Sting had a new band that remained with him for several years. While not totally enamoured of his style of music – give me the Moody Blues any day – I could recognise a hard-working professional at his best. Perhaps to Sting's disappointment, the audience only became really animated when he played some of the old Police hits. To be fair, most of Sting's songs since his Police days have been decidedly down-tempo from those chart-toppers.

The concert went down a storm with the fans and, after several encores, Sting and the band left the stage to rapturous applause, which completely drowned out my booing. With our back-stage passes, the three of us went to greet Sting, along with about 200 others. A seething horde had gathered to give the local lad their best wishes. Friends and relations, local dignitaries and a smattering of Geordie celebs were all jockeying for position. It would have been easier to get an audience with the Pope. Eventually we got to see Sting for a nano-second. He quickly told us to go to his hotel where he would see us for a drink.

Just a select few gathered at Sting's hotel in Gosforth – close friends and relations, with Sting's granny, Agnes, who sadly passed away in 1998, well to the fore. After witnessing the free-for-all circus that went on back-stage, I was well impressed by Sting's patience with all the hangers-on, us included. In the USA, it was even worse apparently as Hollywood stars would barge in and bore his arse off for half an hour and more.

On one famous occasion, Sting's guitarist, Dominic Miller, saw Sting apparently cornered by a guy after a gig in the US, so he thought he would rescue him by saying, 'Hi there, are you in the business?'

The man looked slightly miffed as Sting answered, 'Dominic, he *is* the business!' Dominic had failed to recognise Burt Bacharach.

Despite being in the final stages of fatigue, Sting still managed to stay up most of the night sinking beers until we carried him to bed. The following night, the same ballyhoo resulted after the second concert. Though I hadn't gone to the show, I still turned up for the booze and rustled up two old pals from the past – Tony Hewson and Alan Sutherland.

We talked about the crazy party at Bob Taylor's house when Alan was converted to Catholicism. Bob had been tragically killed in a rail accident and was often in our thoughts, not least because of that bizarre revelry when we were schoolboys. After another night's toping, Sting was off on his travels again, swearing to stay in touch.

More phone calls from far-flung places followed as we neared our mid-life crises – our 40th birthdays. Sting told me that he would be celebrating his with a typically low-key affair in New York's Carnegie Hall in front of 5,000 fans – he was giving a concert that day. Special guests were UB40 (You Be Forty). I had not been invited, though, even if I had, I could not have afforded the plane over as I barely had my bus fare into Newcastle. Besides, what could I have bought him for a present – a pen and pencil set? I don't think so. But I was a bit miffed when I read in the local press that, at this wonderful bash, old friends from way back when had been flown in from all corners of the globe, courtesy of the superstar. No one had flown in from Newcastle, at least none of his old school-pals, so at least he had been even-handed: we could all fuck off.

It was OK for him to phone me at all hours of the night wanting to know the football results, but I was not needed on stage at Carnegie Hall. I had to scrape a few coppers together to buy myself a bottle of Lucozade, while the party-goers were swilling down bottles of chilled Dom Perignon. Did I care? Yes, I fucking well did!

A few days later, he had the temerity to ask how I was getting on. I gave him short shrift. I politely asked him how the party with all his old pals had gone. He became decidedly defensive. He explained away the so-called flying-in of guests by saying there was only one guy that happened to, and Sting had a very good reason for that since he owed him a massive favour. As for the rest of the lads, if he invited one he would have had to invite them all, he argued. I listened in silence before pouncing. I told him I was skint and going down the tubes. If he wanted to make up for this enormous snub, he could always sub me a nice few quid to get me back on the racetrack. An inter-continental groan lodged in my ear. He knew this emotional blackmail would work. He agreed to shore me up and a cheque would be in the post. 'It's only a loan,' Sting insisted.

'Yes, of course it is,' I answered. Missing that party turned out to be a blessing in disguise.

In the event, Sting got a yacht from his record company, A & M, for his birthday. And I got the cost of a yacht back as a loan.

39 – LIVE IN CONCERT: DEATH BY EMBARRASSMENT

Not long after his 40th birthday, Sting was due back on Tyneside as part of yet another world tour. This time it was due to be at the local ice rink in Whitley Bay. At first, I thought that Sting must be going down the pan if he was having to appear in an 'Ice Spectacular', possibly with Torvill and Dean, I fancied.

'I didn't even know you could skate,' I told Sting.

'They cover the fucking ice over, you knacker' was Sting's reply.

'I take it you use roller skates then,' I ventured.

'Yes, that's right, Jim,' he confirmed. Now I was happy.

The day before the concert, Sting, myself and about a hundred other guests were invited to Dave Bradshaw's 40th birthday party at his home in the rural Tyne Valley. All the racing gang and a couple of people I hadn't seen since my school days joined the happy throng. No one knew for sure if the superstar and his girlfriend, now his wife, Trudie Styler, would show up or even find the place for that matter. Sting's sense of direction, or lack of it, is legendary.

Find it, though, they did, and I was introduced to Trudie for the first time with the following words: 'Trudie, this is Jim Berryman. He is a fat bookie-type person. Jim, this is Trudie. She is a slim gorgeous-type person!'

'I'm very pleased to meet you, Trudie. Sting has talked an awful lot about you. I feel like I know you already,' I said.

'And I'm pleased to meet you, Jim. Sting never said a word about you, so you are a complete stranger to me,' she answered with a straight face, before no longer being able to suppress a wicked giggle. 'Only kidding, Jim. Sting has often spoken about you and his old school pals.'

Trudie and I chatted away for a while and I immediately took to her. A very attractive and interesting young woman with a wicked sense of fun, she won me over in minutes. The question was obvious: what the bloody hell did she see in Sting? Whatever it was – it was surely not talent or good looks – they appeared to be perfect foils for each other.

As the drink flowed freely – and in Joe Bulman's case that meant drinking champagne from a pint glass until only his eye-lids could move – I decided to put Sting right with a few home truths. For instance, now that he made a

living writing and singing unfathomable songs, did Sting
still think that he was a better singer than I was? I had
detected no improvement in his voice since we were at
school. As far as I was concerned, nothing had changed. If
you can't sing when you are 12, why should you be any
better at 40? Singers were born not made, I argued to him.
Fortified by ten bottles of Pils, I sincerely informed him
that I could sing any one of his songs better than he could,
especially that one, I told him, when Tammy Wynette had
asked his advice about whether she should seek election to
the Senate or simply become a tailor.

'What the fuck are you rambling on about?' Sting
asked, bemused.

'You know, that song you wrote as your answer,
"Don't stand, sew clothes, Tammy".' Having waited
months to hit him with this, I laughed out loud at him.
I shouldn't have bothered as he only shook his head and
groaned. I went on to tell him that he may have
forgotten, but I was in the school choir and I believed
that he had not quite made it; indeed, he had been frog-
marched out of the hall after his audition. He finally
agreed that I was a better singer than he was (this was
conceded with only the minimum of violence exerted).
We went on to more important matters, such as whether
he knew what the French for 'doleful exhibitionist' was.
I bet Douglas Hesp could have told him.

The party eventually broke up, with me insisting that I
must have ten tickets to the concert complete with back-
stage passes. I couldn't imagine any of us wanting to pay

JAMES BERRYMAN

to see him. Sting muttered back, 'That's fucking well cost me, hasn't it?'

The concert at the ice rink went well. Sitting two rows from the front, I kept my promise to keep a vigilant eye on the floor, making sure that the ice below remained intact. As part of the traditional encores, which were as well-rehearsed as the rest of the show, Sting had decided to wreak revenge for my attack on his singing as well as the bragging about my own warbling ability at Dave's party.

He hushed the 5,000-strong audience, then announced, 'I had now intended to sing, I hope, one of your favourite songs, "Every Breath You Take". However, I have just noticed sitting at the front, an ex-choirboy with a voice of pure velvet. Come on up on stage, Jim, and thrill us all with your version of "Every Breath". Please, audience, give Jim your warmest welcome.' He grinned hideously in my direction, waving me up to join him on stage.

All of the audience around me were looking around for the dulcet-toned crooner in their ranks. As the crowd bayed for me to sing, my friends tried lifting me to my feet. Transfixed with fear, I stood there open-mouthed, my bluff well and truly called. I looked up at the exultant Sting who was still waving me forward, but I pointed to my throat and whispered, 'Laryngitis.'

'It seems that the *meister*-singer has a throat infection, ladies and gentleman. It appears that I will have to sing it myself. Never mind, eh,' he shouted out to further

270

applause, as I burst into a torrent of coughs and wheezes. Sting's victory was apparently complete.

His tomfoolery had not finished for the night either. With the usual vast number of guests shuffling back-stage in the hope of meeting him, including those who wanted to throttle the twat, we were all kept waiting for 15 minutes or so. We were finally ushered forward towards two enormous doors which slowly opened before us. Instead of being led into Sting's dressing-room, however, we found ourselves out in the street. We looked behind us only to see the vast doors shut with a clang. Those looking forward to meeting their hero looked decidedly startled. We merely shrugged our shoulders and made our way to his hotel for a drink.

When we got there, Sting was already sitting with a pint. He had arranged the whole farce himself to his great satisfaction. I managed to explain away my failure to take up his invitation to sing on stage by saying that, if I had sung 'Every Breath You Take', nobody would ever have wanted to hear him sing it again.

As was my wont, I had, in fact, done him a massive favour by this action which would surely save his flagging career. He thanked me profusely for my selfless act. To his total disgust, I then told him that the argument over who had the better voice was still unresolved.

Mick Millar, who was with me, was very supportive. 'So Sting can sing in front of an audience. I bet he couldn't work out a 10 pence Yankee to save his fucking life.' A very good point, well made.

JAMES BERRYMAN

Sting was off the following day on the remainder of his world tour. When he returned, he said I must come and see his new home near Salisbury. I read about it a few days later in the newspapers. It was a mansion, set in acres of countryside. Lake House in Wiltshire was his new abode. I would soon be going there for an auspicious occasion.

40 – STING'S WEDDING AND A GIRLFRIEND CALLED RON

Once again I was flat broke – nay, that's an understatement; I was concave broke. I was routinely sifting through the normal junk mail, final demands, court orders (or should it be 'caught orders'), notice of eviction etc, when I happened upon an exquisite envelope, daintily addressed in the finest copper plate with just a suggestion of an expensive fragrance.

I was about to steam it open when I realised it was addressed to me. I ripped it open. It read:

> Mr James Berryman and Partner
> are cordially invited to the wedding
> of Sting and Trudie
> at the church of St Andrew, Great Durnford
> and private reception in the grounds of
> Lake House.
> On the 21st August 1992
> R.S.V.P.

Good news all round. My longstanding, long-suffering girlfriend would be on holiday at the time. She was gutted, but I would take someone in her place. I thought of selling raffle tickets for the prize, but, when I considered that I could end up with an ugly person who was even poorer than me, I decided against it.

There was no alternative but to invite Ron. He just shaded Sting as a best mate but, to be honest, nobody's going to pay a nickel to read about him, are they? His answer would be – not yet.

A born salesman and keep-fit fanatic – like Sting who's into yoga – Ron worked for, or at least was employed by, a large corporation. Sometimes working up to a 40-hour month (with expenses), he spent so much time in bed his neighbours thought he worked shifts. Anyway he made a decent living and has since gone on to form his own company from which he now makes an indecent living.

Ron accepted the invitation with gusto even though he and Sting had never met. With the RSVP taken care of, the next plan of action concerned the wedding gift. It was a major dilemma: what do you buy the couple with everything for less than fifty quid? It mightn't seem like a lot of money now, but this was in the early 1990s, remember. The answer, of course, was nothing. Ron thought this was a great idea and was all set for the next stage of preparation.

In the end, we didn't have the nerve to go empty-handed, so we eventually bought a framed abstract painting from a part-time milkman friend who knocked them out as a hobby – £40 for cash. As he couldn't draw or paint, he had to do abstracts. Next on the agenda was the hiring of suits.

'Shall we wear black jackets or shall we have white?' we wondered.

'White should only be worn in the tropics, sir,' explained the rather pompous assistant.

'We'll have white then' was Ron's immediate response.

With suits and the gift-wrapped painting in the boot, we headed early for sleepy Wiltshire with Ron at the wheel of his new Merc – what else? – on a bright and sunny Friday.

Sting had arranged our accommodation at a coaching inn, The Red Lion in the nearby city of Salisbury, a nice touch coming from a megastar. Sting once explained to me his predicament concerning such matters. 'If I put my money about, I'm deemed to be flash and, if I don't, I'm a mean bastard.' I suggested a compromise: be a flashy mean bastard. It brought a wry smile.

An uneventful journey saw us arrive at The Lion in the early evening. I telephoned Sting just to confirm our arrival. He sounded in great spirits and invited us over to Lake House for a drink.

After a quick shower and a sharpener in the bar, we were soon entering the grounds of Lake House through a rustic gate, unnoticed by the sparse traffic passing by on what was a very sleepy 'B' road. We travelled about half a mile down a winding single-lane track, with the late-evening sun glinting through the trees. Here and there we saw the occasional security man, easily identified by the amount of sunlight that they blotted out and their general gangsterish demeanour.

Set in acres of stunning English countryside, the mansion that is Lake House was about to have a several-million-pound facelift in keeping with its Grade 'A' listed-building status of course – Sting is no Jockey Wilson. So keen were Sting and Trudie on this, they had decided not to have a honeymoon and, instead, to plough their energies wholeheartedly – as they do with all their projects – into overseeing the renovation.

A couple of limousines and a Range Rover were parked haphazardly on the gravel drive. Armed with the painting, we strode up to the studded oak door. Sting came to the door himself, accompanied by his new bride.

After a ten-year relationship, Sting and Trudie had actually tied the knot two days earlier at Camden Registry Office, a quiet and private affair. Their country blessing on the morrow would turn out to be a spectacular contrast.

There were hugs and passionate embraces all round. Ron was discovering that celebrities hug and embrace. It is only the great unwashed who shake hands or nod cordially. Beckoned to follow, we were led through the oak-panelled, dimly lit reception area and down into the kitchen. For a feel of the inside of Lake House, imagine Oliver Cromwell, Roundheads and Cavaliers, then add dim electricity and you won't be far away.

About a dozen guests were assembled around a long, baronial rectangular table, littered with pewter, crystal and porcelain. A fashion guru, a record producer, a couple of musicians and some old school friends from Newcastle plus their wives sat around the oak table. Some other guests who were also staying at The Lion had missed the cut and were not invited tonight. Those who had made it were still eating a late supper. Everyone seemed to be engaged in conversation, some lightweight and some not so, but everyone was convivial. Sting sat at the top of the table with Trudie; they were obviously still besotted with one another.

The couple opened cards and gifts. Ah! A pair of limited-edition watches from the ill-fated Gianni Versace, Trudie's wedding-dress designer and guest of honour for the big day. Ah! A set of keys. Sting looked puzzled until he realised they were the ignition keys for a brand-new Jaguar car which was nice.

Above the conversation, I heard Sting shout, 'Fenwicks' – a large department store in the centre of Newcastle. I thought, Christ, someone's only gone and bought him Fenwicks! It turned out he was merely commenting on some wrapping paper, which contained a monochrome print of old Newcastle. No milkman originals here, I thought.

We left in time to sink a couple of pints at The Lion, feeling very pleased that the milkman's effort was now hanging in Sting's kitchen in place of a priceless Matisse.

After a long lie-in, a full English breakfast, a trip to the bookie's (we won) and suited and booted, we were ready for the organised coach journey to the church.

The introvert Billy Connolly ensured the journey wasn't dull as we wound our way past throngs of ordinary people doing a bit of celebrity spotting.

The service was like any other, save for the fact that Sting was trussed up like Beau Brummel and Trudie arrived wearing a twenty-grand wedding frock, not to mention the 150 guests packed into the tiny chapel who must have been worth a hundred zillion pounds collectively.

Apart from Gianni Versace and Billy Connolly, guests included 'M' from A & M Records, Pamela Stevenson, Charlotte Rampling with a disgustingly young toy boy in tow who turned out to be her son, Barnaby. Others included Peter Gabriel, Kevin Godley from Godley and Creme. Ron mistakenly thought his name was actually Godley Creme and, at the reception, addressed him casually as Godley all evening. Kevin accepted this treatment through clenched teeth. Members of Sting's old band, The Police, were in attendance and many other celebs were dotted around.

As a romantic gesture, Sting had arranged for Trudie to arrive at the reception on a white horse with Sting leading the way. Another hundred-odd guests showed up at the marquee which was set up in the grounds for the reception.

Champagne flowed in abundance and several hours of eating, drinking, dancing and general merriment followed. A clown was on hand to entertain the younger element.

Reg Presley and the Troggs provided the music with guests joining in. Reg is a neighbour of Sting and they share a common interest in corn circles, though I am more of a Shredded Wheat man myself. On a visit to the Gents, an American high-roller quipped, 'Gee, that Reg Tragg (sic) is something else, isn't he?'

'I couldn't agree more, mate,' I replied.

I had a brief dance with the cheroot-smoking Charlotte Rampling, and I complimented her on her performance in *Oh Mr Porter* co-starring Humphrey Bogart. Unsmiling, she corrected me; it was *The Night Porter* with Dirk Bogarde and, with a last puff of smoke directed at my face, she was off. 'Thank you, *cough*, for the dance *cough*, *cough*, Miss Rampling,' I spluttered.

Ron had made the better choice, rocking and rolling himself into a coma with Pamela Stephenson, while her husband held court in a corner with the cigar-smoking, brandy-drinking brigade to roars of laughter.

Sting and Trudie did the rounds, missing out no one, and then Sting knocked out a few Police classics with his old band-members.

By 4.00am, numbers were beginning to dwindle. We staggered on to the last bus at 5.00am, completely partied out.

On the slow journey back, the bus headlights caught the children's entertainer still in his full clown outfit, thumbing a lift. 'We're not picking THAT fucking clown up, are we?' Godley chirped from the back of the bus to howls of mirth. The dishevelled clown, in need of a shave by now and puffing away on a fag, glumly boarded the bus to more peals of laughter. He was totally bemused. I was totally pissed, Ron was totally asleep and Sting, well, who knows?

41 – RED LETTER DAY

Sting and I were now as close as we had ever been. Maybe he needed someone to call him a useless twat at times, just as I had done at school. Whatever the reason, it was just like old times. We spent weekends together, went racing at Newbury and Ascot and watched our beloved Newcastle United as often as possible.

Although I now call him 'Sting' to his face, I can still distinguish 'Sting' from 'Gordon Sumner'. To me, he will always be 'Sumner', the nervous, cocky, yet vulnerable lad he always was, despite all that has gone before. All his wealth and celebrity are suspended in time when we arse about as if we are still teenagers – I can even forget that he has been awarded an Honorary Degree by the university that I was 'sent down' from some 28 years earlier. However, I still hankered to be back on the racecourse, but getting the funds for yet another assault on the ring was proving difficult. Could I track Sting down?

Curiously, Sting's experiences at the races with us had not put him off horseracing. He must have acquired a taste for the game because he bought some horses in the 1980s. He started at the top and worked his way to the bottom. He must have thought the game was easy when his horse, Sweetcal, won at Brighton at 33/1. And then, with only his second horse Sandalay, he had a winner at Royal Ascot in 1983. Thank God, he was on tour at the time and therefore could not be seen poncing about in top hat and tails sinking Pimms with a bunch of 'Hooray Henrys'. Flushed with success, he paid over £100,000 for a couple of two-year-olds to be trained by Peter Cundell. They both turned out to be useless. Disillusioned, Sting ended his brief flirtation with the Sport of Kings.

When Sting arrived on Tyneside in November 1992 to receive his degree, he informed me that it was no longer me who was the skint one. We were now in the same boat. He had just £3.22 in his bank account, while I had £4.76 in mine. Who would have thought that I would end up richer than Sting? The difference was, of course, that I knew I had £4.76 in my account, whereas Sting was under the impression that he had £5,877,743.22 in his.

He had just received an anonymous letter informing him that his long-time accountant, Keith Moore, whom he had trusted implicitly, had relieved him of several million pounds of his hard-earned cash by investing in Australian curry houses and the like, although he had stopped short of investing in asbestos fire-lighters. When Sting told me, my first reaction was to burst out laughing, just as surely as he would have done if our roles had been reversed.

On reflection, this was not good news, as I was preparing to put the bite on Sting for a good few bob to get back into bookmaking again. Any ideas that I had about getting a loan seemed to be going up in smoke. His bloody accountant hadn't just been fleecing Sting, he had buggered up my plans as well.

I went to the ceremony, held at Newcastle City Hall, as a faculty guest to see Sting receive his Honorary Degree in Music. This mind-numbingly boring ceremony seemed to take ten hours to complete, though it went off without a hitch despite my attempts at a slow handclap. Rooted in his seat for hours on end, Sting sat facing the audience and caught my attention by making gruesome faces at me, though it looked like he was sneering at local dignitaries. He got some hostile looks back in return.

I spoke briefly to him afterwards, but all I could think about was money. I thought that Sting might have been exaggerating his parlous financial position, so I asked him, 'Is this a good time to talk about a loan?' He looked at me with delight. 'Yes, it's a good time, Jim. How much can you afford to lend me?'

I turned on my heel and left the building. With only £4.76 in the bank and my subscription to *Men Only* due, things were looking bleak. Seeing that Keith Moore had apparently purloined Sting's money – though at this time he had not yet been convicted of the offence – it seemed to me that he was a better bet for a loan than Sting was.

I drafted a letter to Mr Moore, informing him that, although he did not know me personally, we had a mutual friend who apparently had the IQ of a lemming. As he now had a good wedge of Sting's cash, some of which Sting would have undoubtedly loaned me, it was only fair that he should put some of it my way.

Reading the letter over, I realised that it just might have been construed as attempted blackmail. I didn't intend to be sharing a cell with him, just some of Sting's cash. Pursuing the blackmail theme, I could have said that, if he did not come up with the dosh, I would get the law on to him, but in the event some stupid bastard beat me to it.

I had been drifting in and out of jobs with other bookmakers and, at one time, I actually owned a betting shop with a partner, Dave Burns. Dave was yet another old boy from St Cuthbert's, who incidentally once let in three goals direct from corners in one match while playing for the school team, a feat that surely should be recorded in *The Guinness Book of Records*. We never made any money because the social club next to our shop seemed to be populated by the most inspired punters the betting world has ever seen.

Whatever I did, even backed by Sting's cash and moral support, turned to shit. I had reached the end of the line. I became a statistic: Jim Berryman, actor, comedian, bookie and lounge lizard, was on the dole!

By now, I was an expert at signing on, which was, and still can be, a very demeaning experience. You see all of those poor young people with expressionless faces, talking in monosyllables and without a hint of hope in their dead eyes – the dregs of humanity, barely scratching a living. And that was just the staff!

Nobody had a position for a fortysomething fat, ex-bookie. What else could I do? I went on a training course to learn new skills as a computer operator and I had been there a fortnight before any of the instructors spoke to me. Even then it was to tell me I hadn't done enough work and that, if I did not apply myself better, I would never learn how to drive a forklift truck. I responded by telling the man that I didn't think I would win the Eurovision Song Contest either and politely asked him what that had to do with computer operating. I had been in the wrong building. After a week of computer training, I applied to go on the forklift truck course. The staff there were institutionalised with canoe-sized chips on their shoulders. I resigned my commission after a couple of bleak weeks.

I was unemployable. Life had dealt me rotten cards that I had played extremely badly. One morning, not my usual time of day, a buff envelope landed on my mat. My heart leaped. I had obviously been underpaid by the Department of Social Security, possibly for months, and this was a big fat giro making up for the shortfall. I ripped open the envelope. I was right; it was that thing that is green and white and can get you pissed – a DSS cheque. I scanned it to find its value: £200 possibly, £300

I hoped. There it was in words and figures. I had received a Giro for '1p' – one fucking penny! I wept bitterly. I phoned the Benefit Office to query the amount, but it was correct. Though I was tempted I didn't cash it in, so at least the man in the post office would not need to ask me how I would like the cash. My finances were non-existent. Borrowing was no solution, even if I found anyone daft enough to lend me the cash. Those closest to me rallied round, including Sting, though I did not let him know just how broke I was. It wasn't much consolation that Sting was also approaching bankruptcy, if his accountant Keith Moore had anything to do with it. Moore's trial was soon in the headlines.

42 – WITLESS FOR THE PROSECUTION

It seems incomprehensible that someone can have over £5 million spirited away from them without their knowledge. No matter how wealthy the individual, it just doesn't seem possible. Nobody who has amassed that sort of cash could possibly be an idiot, but to lose that amount and not know then you must be an idiot – a sort of Catch 5 Mil situation.

Sting found himself facing exactly this conundrum. His accountant, Keith Moore, had redistributed over £5 million of his wealth without his knowledge. He had trusted him implicitly, which meant there was no need to check his bank balance 'every five minutes,' or so said Sting in his defence.

The public perception of this situation, I fancy, is that losing that amount of money is God's way of telling Sting he had far too much of the stuff in the first place and that

287

he could have avoided any problem by giving it all away to his close friends. Well, that's my story and I'm sticking to it!

What Sting failed to mention was that he had over one hundred separate bank accounts that Mr Moore could make use of. Sympathy, if there ever had been any at all for Sting's plight, was on the wane.

Keith Moore was being paid a salary in the region of £800,000 per annum to look after Sting's affairs but apparently it was not enough and he wanted more. It's clear that, if you are paid that sort of salary, then you can't be an idiot. However, if you filch £5 million from a client and invest it in ex-Russian army aeroplanes and curry houses in Australia, then surely you must be an idiot. Catch 5 Mil again.

Keith Moore's investments had gone down the Swanee and one of the auditors of his firm believed that Sting knew nothing of the deception and wrote to him with his findings. And of course he was right. Sting had no idea that Moore had been using his money in such an investment-sapping manner. Not unnaturally, Sting was horrified and confronted his errant accountant.

Moore insisted that the investments were made in Sting's best interests and it was just bad luck that they had failed. Sting called in the police, who arrested the accountant and charged him with theft.

Moore denied the charges, insisting that he had power of attorney over Sting's money. Sting's bankers, Coutts, also insisted that they were not at fault, despite the fact that no mandates were ever found allowing Moore unrestricted access to Sting's funds. Sting threatened legal action for recovery of the lost money, which was eventually repaid in full.

Proving this fact, a giant cheque, like those that lottery winners brandish in newspaper photographs, was framed and mounted on the toilet wall of Sting's London home for several years.

The criminal trial was heard at Southwark Crown Court in south London. A couple of days before Sting was due to give evidence for the prosecution, the phone rang at my home in Newcastle. It was Sting. He asked me if I fancied coming down to The Smoke for a few days while the trial was on. Although trials at Crown Court aren't exactly spectator sports, I quite fancied a look at the proceedings and, besides, I could hardly turn him down in his moment of need. His motive for asking me could only have been that he saw me as a cheerleader or chief mourner should the verdict not go his way. Whatever happened, I was off down south.

After a quiet night, I was woken with a raucous 'Call James Berryman'. Sting howled at me from the bottom of the stairs in mock courtroom style. Over breakfast I peppered Sting with 'I put it to you, Mister Sumner, you have more money than sense and deserve to lose all your cash' plus a few more choice phrases such as 'I suggest to you that it is you who should be on trial for impersonating a rock star.'

He seemed in good spirits when we left for the court,

driven by his long-time 'do everything else for Sting but sing' Billy Francis. As we neared the court building, the snappers were waiting. Paparazzi, TV and radio all milled together in a huge scrum. Billy went straight into court, while I slipped out of the back door before attempting to take my place in the public gallery. Sting dutifully stood there glum-faced – no change there, then – while they snapped away, studiously refusing to answer questions like 'What's it like to be skint, Sting?'

I was slipping into the court building to queue for the public gallery, when I was approached by a young woman who looked vaguely familiar. 'Triona Holden, BBC,' she shouted. 'Could you tell me, are you Miles Copeland?' Miles was Sting's manager at the time. He is an American and slim with a shock of white hair. I looked nothing like him.

'No, I'm not.'

'It's just that I saw you get out of the limo with Sting and his driver.'

'I'm just a friend of his, that's all,' I replied, noticing that a girl standing next to her was feverishly sketching me on a large notepad.

'Court artist,' explained Triona to my bemusement.

When I relayed the story about being mistaken for Miles Copeland later to Sting and Billy, Billy laughed, telling me that I should have answered with the line: 'No, I'm not him. If you cut me, I would bleed!'

We shuffled into the impressive courtroom, which had rows of press benches and a decent-sized public gallery.

The dock, however, was enormous. Used years earlier for IRA terrorist trials, it looked like a large office bounded on four sides by thick, bullet-proof glass. This Keith Moore must be more dangerous than I thought...

The air was suddenly split with a cry of 'All rise' as his honour sidled in, accepting the bows from the assembled briefs.

I was sitting near the aisle with only room left for one person to sit next to me, so I spread myself out to get more comfortable – this could be a very long day.

The usher cried out, 'Call Gordon Sumner.'

All eyes turned to the back of the court as the usher opened the door to the ante-chamber. 'Here's the greedy fucker now,' a voice boomed out from behind me in the public gallery to a few titters from the public area, though no one else in the court could hear because of all that glass directly in front of us.

Sting was led in by the lady usher, who pointed in the direction of the witness box before turning to her right. For some inexplicable reason, Sting ignored her instruction and, on seeing me, slipped in and sat next to me, forcing the rest of the row to bunch up.

'Cunt,' said the voice from behind.

'What are you doing?' I implored, to a shrug from the pop star.

The usher turned around and, instead of seeing Sting securely positioned in the witness box, she was alarmed to note that he had apparently vanished into thin air. She retraced her steps to the rear of the court, looking all over for the errant star, who was engaged with me in a barging match as I attempted to push him into the aisle. The usher, defeated, walked back into court, seemingly ready to tell the judge the idiot had scarpered. Finally I won the tug of war and Sting reappeared behind the usher, much to her amazement. It looked like he had pulled off a masterful illusion. I was expecting a round of applause.

'Wanker,' cried the voice from behind.

The questioning of Sting was boring in the extreme and the voice behind me went into overdrive. I had looked back several times to try and see who this moron could be but everyone was silent, though I had my suspicions. There was a dishevelled-looking character two rows behind; his arms were folded and he was staring into space. This must be him, I mused. I wasn't wrong.

There were two young Asian ladies sitting in front of me who became the next target of the loony behind.

'Fucking black bitches,' he ranted. No one in the gallery did anything but tut. Back in Newcastle, someone would have nutted him by now. I finally snapped.

'Shut your foul mouth or I will have you thrown out,' I called out, turning my head in his direction and looking tough, or so I thought.

'Fuck off, nigger-lover,' he kindly replied.

I was steaming. I stood up and tried to get into his row. All sense had gone from my brain as I tried to get to him.

'I'll knock your fucking head off,' I swore as fellow members of the gallery restrained me.

The loony sat there unmoved as I noticed the two Asian girls leaving the gallery. I ceased my attempt to get myself arrested and joined them outside.

We approached a constable and told him of the situation, fully expecting him to arrest the idiot but he said he had no jurisdiction in the court. We would have to wait for a recess at which point he could inform the judge who had summary powers to jail the loony for contempt.

I looked forward to that but in the event it never happened as the cracker slipped unnoticed from the court some time later.

I was beginning to play 'I spy with my little eye' with myself to alleviate the boredom during the afternoon session, which was only lightened by the judge referring to Sting as 'the accused' on a couple of occasions to howls of derision from the press gallery.

The rest of Sting's testimony appeared to be simply about whether or not he knew that Moore had invested his money without his knowledge. Repetition was the name of the game – I will not repeat myself. I repeat. I will not repeat myself. Then things took an almost Perry Masonish turn.

The defence announced, 'I suggest to you, Mister Sumner, that this email clearly states that Mr Moore informed you of his investment plans.'

The brief waved the document grandly in the air for

all to see. Sting looked at the paper before declaring,
'No, sir. It does not...' in his 'I'm not just a singer but an
actor as well' voice. 'This is not, nor has it ever been, my
email address.'

'No more questions,' the crestfallen brief mumbled.

Sting had had his day in court and Keith Moore got a
good few more days than just one in jail.

Needless to say, the press gave Sting a lot of stick. He
had so much dosh he didn't even notice the loss of £5m
etc, etc, but that still didn't give Moore the right to
purloin his money. No, if anyone should have nicked
his hard-earned, it should have been someone much
nearer to home. Make your own choice who that
should have been...

43 – MASTER AND COMMANDER

Sting wasn't triumphant at the jailing of Keith Moore. He was even a little sad since this was a man whom he had known and trusted for years, but justice was seen to be done and life went on, even for Mr Moore. More albums, films and world tours followed – for Sting, not Moore – and his reputation within the industry and his fortune both grew and he is now recognised as one of the grand old men of pop and one of the richest artistes in the world.

Yes, this is my old mate, Gordon Sumner. Hard to believe, but am I grudging about his success? You bet your arse I am! I'm a better singer than he is and I have got loads more hair, yet he owns more properties across the world than I own dinner plates. But I forgive him.

I once asked him, as we were strolling around his palatial grounds at Lake House, how he squared the fact that he was so wealthy with the fact that there were people who would not be eating anything for a week: the poor and starving people of the world versus the splendour of his life. Was he embarrassed by it? He had obviously thought about it before because he answered almost immediately that, should his wealth disappear or even if it were given to the disadvantaged for redistribution, there would still be lots of poor, starving people in the world. He could change nothing, he reckoned, though I mused there might be someone on a Rwanda rubbish tip wearing gold-lamé trousers and a Versace string vest.

Sting was beginning to stack up awards from around the globe and for a while appeared to be a professional award and party/premiere-goer. His honorary Masters Degree in Music from Northumbria University was specially well received particularly as this is the only way the tone-deaf twat could ever have got a degree! I know that he always fancied an Oscar – no, not for acting, don't be daft! I mean for a song – and he was nominated three times, turned up three times and three times he sat there with a face like a bastard cat when some other old fart was given the award. Randy Newman? Give me a break! Sting will get one some day, of that I'm sure because he has never failed musically before. All right, I forgot about *The Beggar's Opera* (or was that *The Threepenny Opera*?). Ironically, he came closest in 2004 when his next-door neighbour Annie Lennox won the prize!

I used to tease him that, while some of his contemporaries like Dame Elton John and pretend 'Sir' Bob Geldof were honoured by Her Majesty, he would have to remain Sting OBE – Overlooked Because of Ecstasy.

Sting's call for the decriminalisation of so-called recreational drugs met with the greatest public criticism he has ever encountered – apart from his singing obviously. His point that you can't stop young people taking drugs like 'E', so you might as well make sure that the end product is pure and therefore regulate the production and supply of the drug was not terribly well received – not by the parents of dead teenagers who had perished taking the drug anyway – and he was roundly shouted down by the media.

Sting has a large family himself and would be devastated if anything should befall his own kids. He was hurt by the criticism, mainly because he certainly was not advocating the taking of drugs – been there, done that, had the therapy – but rather that more controls should be put in place to protect drug-takers. A little bit of politics there, folks. Whatever the case, it seemed that an honour would not be coming his way. We were all wrong.

In 2003 Sting was awarded a CBE, Commander of the British Empire no less. He had gone from playing non-League to the Premiership in one season! I've never been sure who actually has the final say on these awards, though along with the Queen and the Prime Minister I think Jimmy Saville has the casting vote. Don't ask me why, it's just a feeling I've got.

Needless to say, a celebration was in order and a luncheon bash was organised for a hundred guests on the day of the investiture. My invitation for the thrash at Harry's Bar in Mayfair was suitably vague – 'Dress, smart, casual or scruffy'. That seemed to cover just about everyone providing that Jonathan Ross wasn't invited. The usual suspects from the Newcastle area were to be flown down to The Smoke for the occasion. Sting's office as usual would make sure everything went according to plan and Sting's sister Angela did her usual brilliant job.

The Newcastle mob were just about the first guests to arrive. Who says there is no such thing as a free lunch! We stood on the terrace supping peach blinis at a rare rate of knots before the great man turned up, still wearing his 'claw-hammer' coat and with his CBE wrapped tightly around his neck. Sting warmly embraced the first of his guests before arriving in front of me. He stood back in mock (I hope) horror, looking me up and down and muttering, 'Fucking hell, Berryman, I know the invite said "scruffy" but for God's sake, man!'

I smiled weakly and only just managed, 'Oh fuck off, Dracula' by way of reply before he was whisked away to greet the rest of the throng. After a lunch of wild mushrooms (roughly the same as tame ones), sea bass (fish without batter) and risotto (Ambrosia creamed rice) followed by a truly scrumptious pudding (ice cream), the good, the bad and the ugly gave speeches to honour their host.

Sir Ian McKellen, 'Sir' Bob Geldof and Lord Jimmy Nail of Byker all spoke with varying degrees of sycophancy: Sir Ian, a lot, 'Sir' Bob, none at all, and Lord Nail, just the right amount. Indeed, Jimmy spoke with real warmth about Sting and the North-East and got the loudest round of applause, mainly because we Geordies are a rowdy lot at the best of times.

Sting replied with his tongue very firmly in his cheek, claiming that now he has the same rank as James Bond, the government might be able to use his talents in far-reaching ways. After all, he did travel the world and could have as many beautiful women as he wanted, except he didn't want any and he is as much use at fighting as he is at singing. All in all, a grand time was had by all and, after a champagne-hazed flight back to bonny Newcastle, we returned to the real world.

Sting was still touring and on the agenda was a gig at the Newcastle Arena. But just before the concert, he was laid low with laryngitis. Who says there isn't a god? On the same day, the Variety Club of Great Britain bestowed on Sting yet another honour and yet another lunch, with wall-to-wall celebrities from the area – and me. In the VIP Lounge prior to lunch, I mixed easily with the celebs until I met my all-time hero, Alan Shearer, Newcastle United's captain, the Lion of Gosforth himself. Using Sting as my foil – he comes in handy sometimes – I managed to get a one-on-one with my hero, hoping against hope that Hughie McBride would come in, see me with Alan and be eaten up with jealousy. After only a couple of minutes of me boring the arse off Alan, Hughie arrived. I smiled malevolently towards him. 'Yes, Hughie, this is me and Alan friggin' Shearer! What do you think of that?' I mused but didn't say. Then you could have knocked me down with a stotty cake as Shearer turned to Hughie with an enormous grin and cried, 'Hughie! How lovely to see you and Paddy [Hughie's wife]. You look wonderful!!'

I felt physically sick. How in the name of craw's cacky did Hughie McBride and spouse know Alan Shearer? I sidled away unnoticed, ate my lunch at a table full of strangers and slipped off home before it turned out Hughie was Mark Knopfler's bosom buddy as well. I ended the proceedings by drunkenly telling actor Tim Healy that it was only my presence stopping him from being the least famous person in the room. In fairness, I think he gets a lot of that.

Short of a knighthood and beatification, there isn't much left for Sting to be awarded with. Indeed, it has just been announced that Sting is to be made a Freeman of the City of Newcastle. I'm not too sure what that entails but I think it means they can never put you in jail there and you can drive your swine and Ferrari over the town moor without fear or favour. Sting is one of the few people I know who actually herds swine, so this could be a real boon when the public have had enough of his caterwauling.

Sting and I don't see as much of each other as we used to – at school that was a lot – but I love him like a brother and always will. I was at dinner with him at Lake House not so long ago and I was doing my usual piss-taking when Andrea, an Italian flautist friend of Sting's who perhaps did not see the irony behind my ribbing, challenged me to say what I really thought of the Lord of the Manor.

'I'm incredibly proud of what this man has achieved in his life but nowhere near as proud as I am to call him my friend,' I answered without even thinking.

'Oh, you old sweetie,' Sting replied before guiding me through to the music room where he joined me in howling out 'If I Loved You' from the musical *Carousel*. You can't buy moments like that.